D1708486

PROUDLY DESIGNED ON THE UPPER WEST SIDE
(OF KANSAS CITY).

BUILD YOUR
BAR FROM SCRATCH

BAR×NONE

ONE DRINK AT
A TIME

START OUT WITH 2 INGREDIENTS,
END UP WITH AN UNLICENSED BARTENDING DEGREE.

DISCLAIMER

X X X

LOOK, WE TRIED OUR BEST.

WE'RE JUST A COUPLE OF DESIGNERS THAT
LOVE TO DRINK. WE ALSO HAPPEN TO HAVE A
WEIRD AFFINITY FOR INFOGRAPHICS, USELESS
TRIVIA, AND NEEDLESSLY PUTTING OURSELVES
THROUGH HELL. HENCE, THE BOOK THAT YOU'RE
HOLDING IN YOUR HANDS.

THAT SAID, COCKTAIL HISTORY IS HAZY AT
BEST...AND THERE ARE THOUSANDS OF WAYS TO
MAKE THESE DRINKS. SO CUT US SOME SLACK.
WE'RE BOUND TO HAVE MADE A FEW MISTAKES,
EVEN THOUGH WE TRIED REALLY HARD NOT TO.

ANYWAY, WE HOPE YOU ENJOY IT. THIS
COCKTAIL BOOK WAS A LABOR OF LOVE...THEN
HATRED...THEN LOVE AGAIN.

P.S. DRINK RESPONSIBLY (PLEASE)

HOW TO USE THIS BOOK

LET'S GET STARTED:

EVER OPEN UP A COCKTAIL BOOK, PICK A DRINK TO MAKE, AND
QUIT AFTER YOU SEE A LIST OF 5 INGREDIENTS THAT YOU
DON'T HAVE? US TOO. THAT'S WHY THIS ONE IS DIFFERENT.

HERE'S HOW IT WORKS:

THIS BOOK IS BEST USED (THE FIRST TIME ANYWAY) BY STARTING
WITH THE INITIAL DRINK AND WORKING YOUR WAY THROUGH IN
ORDER. YOU'LL START WITH A SIMPLE 2 INGREDIENT COCKTAIL,
AND EACH CONSECUTIVE DRINK WILL ADD A MAXIMUM OF ONE
NEW INGREDIENT.* BY THE END, YOU'LL HAVE A FULLY STOCKED
BAR AND 190 COCKTAILS IN YOUR REPERTOIRE.

> *FYI, WE'RE NOT COUNTING LEMONS, LIMES, & OTHER GROCERY STUFF.
> WE ALWAYS CALL THEM OUT AT THE TOP OF EACH DRINK, THOUGH.

SUPPLIES YOU'LL NEED (SOME MORE THAN OTHERS)

☐ COCKTAIL SHAKER   MEASURING SPOONS ☐

☐ MIXING GLASS*   JIGGER / MEASURING CUPS ☐

☐ STRAINER*   HAND WHISK ☐

☐ MUDDLER   HAND & UPRIGHT BLENDER ☐

> *YOU CAN USE A SHAKER INSTEAD IF YOU WANT. USE THE BOTTOM HALF AS
> A MIXING GLASS, STIR, & PUT THE LID BACK ON. VOILÀ, A STRAINER.

HERE'S HOW TO MAKE A TWIST (WE'LL DO IT A LOT)

FIRST, CUT OFF A STRIP OF THE PEEL. NEXT ZEST (AKA SCRAPE)
THE SURFACE. NOW JUST TWIST IT OVER THE GLASS, RUB IT ON
THE RIM, AND DROP IT IN.

HOW TO USE THIS BOOK

WHY ALL THE PICTURES?

BECAUSE THEY'RE FUN TO LOOK AT, AND WE THINK IT'S USEFUL
TO SEE A QUICK VISUAL REFERENCE OF WHAT YOU'RE MAKING.

NOTE: THE SIZING OF THE MEASUREMENTS ARE APPROXIMATE,
AND THE INGREDIENTS ARE ONLY COLOR CODED PER DRINK. IN
OTHER WORDS, DON'T TAKE THEM TOO LITERALLY.

*BTW, A SPLASH IS MORE THAN A DASH, BUT BOTH IMPLY THAT
YOU CAN USE MORE (OR LESS) TO YOUR OWN TASTE.

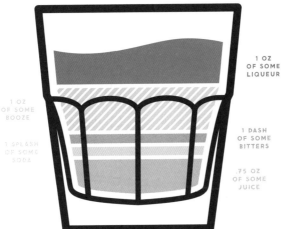

1 OZ
OF SOME
LIQUEUR

1 OZ
OF SOME
BOOZE

1 DASH
OF SOME
BITTERS

1 SPLASH
OF SOME
SODA

.75 OZ
OF SOME
JUICE

IF YOUR DRINK LOOKS LIKE OURS, YOU'VE HAD TOO MANY.

LIQUOR & MIXER INVENTORY

JUST CHECK THEM OFF AS YOU GO:

☐ THIS IS AN ALCOHOL   ☐ THIS IS A MIXER

SEE THOSE ASTERISKS? THEY EXPIRE QUICKER...SO GET DRINKING.

☐ DRY GIN   ☐ GENEVER GIN
☐ CLUB SODA*   ☐ TABASCO SAUCE
☐ TONIC WATER*   ☐ SUGAR CUBES
☐ ANGOSTURA BITTERS   ☐ SWEET VERMOUTH*
☐ PASTIS   ☐ OLD TOM GIN
☐ DRY VERMOUTH*   ☐ HONEY
☐ ORANGE BITTERS   ☐ GINGER ALE*
☐ ORGEAT*   ☐ VODKA
☐ FINO SHERRY*   ☐ TRIPLE SEC
☐ SIMPLE SYRUP*   ☐ LILLET BLANC*
☐ LIME JUICE   ☐ GALLIANO
☐ LEMON JUICE   ☐ DARK RUM
☐ MARASCHINO LIQUEUR   ☐ WHITE RUM
☐ RASPBERRY LIQUEUR   ☐ GRAPEFRUIT JUICE*
☐ CHAMPAGNE*   ☐ BLANCO TEQUILA
☐ ORANGE JUICE*   ☐ RYE WHISKEY
☐ ABSINTHE   ☐ RED WINE*
☐ GRENADINE*   ☐ COGNAC
☐ CREAM*   ☐ CURAÇAO
☐ TENNESSEE WHISKEY   ☐ CAMPARI

LIQUOR & MIXER INVENTORY

- [ ] PROSECCO*
- [ ] ANISETTE LIQUEUR
- [ ] COFFEE LIQUEUR
- [ ] PINEAPPLE JUICE*
- [ ] MELON LIQUEUR
- [ ] COCA-COLA*
- [ ] GINGER BEER*
- [ ] DUBONNET ROUGE*
- [ ] PEACH LIQUEUR
- [ ] APPLE JUICE*
- [ ] BRANDY
- [ ] BOURBON
- [ ] PEYCHAUD'S BITTERS
- [ ] SCOTCH
- [ ] CRANBERRY JUICE*
- [ ] SOUR MIX
- [ ] CACHAÇA
- [ ] ORANGE LIQUEUR
- [ ] ROSE WATER
- [ ] AGAVE NECTAR
- [ ] CRÈME DE CASSIS*
- [ ] PASSION FRUIT JUICE*
- [ ] HONEY SYRUP*
- [ ] SAKÉ

- [ ] REPOSADO TEQUILA
- [ ] BÉNÉDICTINE
- [ ] LEMON-LIME SODA*
- [ ] OLIVE JUICE*
- [ ] AMONTILLADO SHERRY
- [ ] AMARETTO
- [ ] ELDERFLOWER LIQUEUR
- [ ] PEACH PUREE*
- [ ] TOMATO JUICE*
- [ ] ORANGE FLOWER WATER
- [ ] WORCESTERSHIRE SAUCE
- [ ] FERNET
- [ ] IRISH WHISKEY
- [ ] GREEN CHARTREUSE
- [ ] HORSERADISH SAUCE*
- [ ] LEMON SODA*
- [ ] COLD BREW COFFEE*
- [ ] PISCO
- [ ] CITRUS VODKA
- [ ] PX SHERRY*
- [ ] STOUT BEER*
- [ ] COCONUT RUM
- [ ] ALLSPICE DRAM

*HOW LONG DO THEY STAY FRESH?
YOU SHOULD GOOGLE THAT.

TO GET STARTED, YOU JUST NEED:

■ DRY GIN (PICK SOMETHING GOOD AND JUNIPERY)

■ AND SOME CLUB SODA

OH, AND MAKE SURE YOU HAVE A LIME

FOR ANY LITERATURE/DRINKING BUFFS OUT THERE, THIS DRINK APPEARS IN CHAPTER 7 OF 'THE GREAT GATSBY.'

INGREDIENTS

■ 2 OZ DRY GIN

■ 4 OZ CLUB SODA

■ LIME (GARNISH)

INSTRUCTIONS

GET SERVING GLASS ☐

FILL WITH ICE ☐

ADD FIRST INGREDIENT ☐

SQUEEZE IN HALF LIME ☐

DROP LIME INTO GLASS ☐

TOP W/ CLUB SODA ☐

STIR TO COMBINE ☐

WHAT DO YOU THINK?

. . . .

. . . .

DRINK THIS AGAIN?   YES ☐   NO ☐   IF DESPERATE ☐

BONUS TRIVIA

CREATED IN THE 1890s AT A WASHINGTON D.C. BAR CALLED 'SHOEMAKER'S,' THIS COCKTAIL WAS CONCEIVED BY, AND NAMED AFTER, THE PROMINENT LOBBYIST (AND DRINKER) COLONEL 'JOE' RICKEY.

HE ACTUALLY PREFERRED HIS ORIGINAL VERSION, USING RYE WHISKEY INSTEAD OF GIN, BUT THE GIN RICKEY BECAME CONSIDERABLY MORE POPULAR.

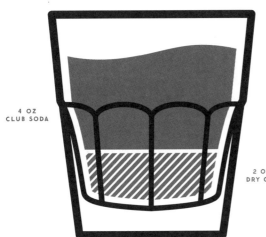

4 OZ
CLUB SODA

2 OZ
DRY GIN

WE'D RECOMMEND A LOWBALL GLASS FOR THIS ONE.

FIRST THINGS FIRST, GO BUY SOME:

☐ TONIC WATER

OH, AND YOU'LL ALSO NEED A LIME OR TWO

THE NON-OFFICIAL DRINK OF BRASS MONKEY. WE'D MAKE IT OFFICIAL, BUT WE DON'T KNOW WHERE TO DO THAT.

INGREDIENTS

- 2 OZ DRY GIN
- TONIC WATER
- LIME (GARNISH)

INSTRUCTIONS

GET SERVING GLASS ☐
FILL WITH ICE ☐
ADD FIRST 2 INGREDIENTS ☐
TOP W/ TONIC WATER ☐
STIR TO COMBINE ☐
GARNISH W/ LIME WEDGE ☐

WHAT DO YOU THINK?

. . . .

. . . .

. . . .

DRINK THIS AGAIN?   YES ☐   NO ☐   IF DESPERATE ☐

IN THE 1700s, QUININE (IN TONIC) WAS USED TO TREAT MALARIA. THE GIN WAS ADDED TO MASK THE BITTERNESS.

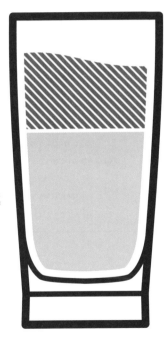

2 OZ
DRY GIN

TONIC
WATER

YOU SHOULD PROBABLY USE A HIGHBALL GLASS.

FIRST THINGS FIRST, GO BUY SOME:

ANGOSTURA BITTERS

OH, AND MAKE SURE YOU HAVE A LEMON

THE RECIPE FOR ANGOSTURA BITTERS IS RUMORED TO CONTAIN 40+ INGREDIENTS, BUT ONLY 5 PEOPLE KNOW.

INGREDIENTS

2 OZ DRY GIN
4 DASH ANGOSTURA BITTERS
LEMON (GARNISH)

INSTRUCTIONS

CHILL SERVING GLASS ☐
ADD & SWIRL BITTERS ☐
DISCARD BITTERS ☐
GET MIXING GLASS & ADD ICE ☐
POUR IN GIN & STIR UNTIL CHILLED ☐
STRAIN INTO GLASS ☐
GARNISH W/ LEMON TWIST ☐

WHAT DO YOU THINK?

. . . .

. . . .

DRINK THIS AGAIN?   YES ☐   NO ☐   IF DESPERATE ☐

BONUS TRIVIA

THE DISTINCTIVE LABEL ON ANGOSTURA BITTERS WAS REALLY
A MISTAKE. DUE TO MISCOMMUNICATION, THE LABEL WAS MADE
TOO BIG, BUT THERE WAS NO TIME TO FIX IT.

2 OZ
DRY GIN

4 DASH
ANGOSTURA
BITTERS

USE A COUPE GLASS. TRUST US, IT'S WORTH IT.

FIRST THINGS FIRST, GO BUY SOME:

☐ PASTIS (IT'S PRONOUNCED PA-S̄TEES, BTW)

OH, AND YOU'LL ALSO NEED ANOTHER LEMON

FOG FORMS WHEN THE DIFFERENCE BETWEEN THE DEW POINT & THE TEMPERATURE OF THE AIR IS LESS THAN 4°F.

INGREDIENTS

INSTRUCTIONS

☐ 1.75 OZ DRY GIN

☐ .5 OZ PASTIS

☐ LEMON (GARNISH)

GET MIXING GLASS & ADD ICE ☐

ADD ALL INGREDIENTS ☐

STIR UNTIL CHILLED ☐

GET SERVING GLASS ☐

FILL WITH ICE ☐

STRAIN INTO GLASS ☐

GARNISH W/ LEMON TWIST ☐

WHAT DO YOU THINK?

. . . .

. . . .

. . . .

. . . .

DRINK THIS AGAIN?   YES ☐   NO ☐   IF DESPERATE ☐

BONUS TRIVIA

THIS DRINK IS RUMORED TO HAVE BEEN BURGESS MERIDITH'S GO-TO HANGOVER CURE. YOU KNOW, MICKEY FROM 'ROCKY.'

ALSO RUMORED: BURGESS BELIEVED THAT A DOLPHIN CALLED TO HIM TELEPATHICALLY FOR HELP IN THE MIDDLE OF THE NIGHT WHILE STAYING AT A FRIEND'S HOUSE ON THE BEACH. HE RAN OUT AND FOUND A DOLPHIN CAUGHT IN A NET UNDER A DOCK. HE RELEASED IT, SAVING ITS LIFE.

1.75 OZ
DRY GIN

.5 OZ
PASTIS

WE'D RECOMMEND A LOWBALL GLASS FOR THIS ONE.

FIRST THINGS FIRST, GO BUY SOME:

DRY VERMOUTH

OH, AND YOU'LL ALSO NEED A PICKLED ONION

A FAVORITE OF SANDRA BULLOCK'S CHARACTER IN 'THE NET.' THE DRINK IS BETTER THAN THE MOVIE.

INGREDIENTS

INSTRUCTIONS

INGREDIENTS	INSTRUCTIONS
2.5 OZ DRY GIN	GET SHAKER & ADD ICE ☐
.5 OZ DRY VERMOUTH	ADD ALL INGREDIENTS ☐
PICKLED ONION (GARNISH)	SHAKE UNTIL CHILLED ☐
	STRAIN INTO GLASS ☐
	GARNISH W/ PICKLED ONION ☐

WHAT DO YOU THINK?

. . . .

. . . .

. . . .

. . . .

DRINK THIS AGAIN?   YES ☐   NO ☐   IF DESPERATE ☐

BONUS TRIVIA

IN 1968, MEL GIBSON'S FATHER WON $4,680 ON JEOPARDY.

.5 OZ DRY
VERMOUTH

2.5 OZ
DRY GIN

THIS ONE DEFINITELY CALLS FOR A MARTINI GLASS.

FIRST THINGS FIRST, GO BUY SOME:

☐ ORANGE BITTERS

YOU CAN USE AN OLIVE INSTEAD OF A LEMON TWIST (IF YOU MUST)

REPORTEDLY A FAVORITE OF THE ROYAL FAMILY
(HYPOTHESIS: THEY'RE THE SECRET TO LONG LIFE).

INGREDIENTS	INSTRUCTIONS
2 OZ DRY GIN	GET MIXING GLASS ☐
1 OZ DRY VERMOUTH	FILL WITH ICE ☐
1 DASH ORANGE BITTERS	ADD ALL INGREDIENTS ☐
LEMON (GARNISH)	STIR UNTIL CHILLED ☐
	STRAIN INTO SERVING GLASS ☐
	GARNISH W/ LEMON TWIST ☐

WHAT DO YOU THINK?

. . . .

. . . .

. . . .

DRINK THIS AGAIN?　　　YES ☐　　NO ☐　　IF DESPERATE ☐

BONUS TRIVIA

MOST BARTENDERS SAY THAT MARTINIS SHOULD ACTUALLY BE
STIRRED (NOT SHAKEN) FOR THE BEST COMBINATION.

2 OZ
DRY GIN

1 OZ DRY
VERMOUTH

1 DASH
ORANGE
BITTERS

MARTINI GLASSES ARE, WELL, MEANT FOR MARTINIS.

FIRST THINGS FIRST, GO BUY SOME:

☐ ORGEAT (IT'S OR-ZHAAT IN CASE YOU'RE WONDERING)

DON'T FORGET TO ADD THIS TO YOUR INVENTORY LIST

> FYI: ORGEAT IS A SWEET SYRUP MADE FROM ALMONDS, SUGAR, & ROSE (OR ORANGE) FLOWER WATER.

INGREDIENTS

INSTRUCTIONS

☐ 1 OZ ABSINTHE

☐ 1 OZ ORGEAT

☐ WATER

GET SERVING GLASS & ADD ICE ☐

ADD FIRST 2 INGREDIENTS ☐

TOP W/ WATER TO TASTE ☐

WHAT DO YOU THINK?

. . . .

. . . .

. . . .

. . . .

. . . .

. . . .

DRINK THIS AGAIN? YES ☐ NO ☐ IF DESPERATE ☐

WHAT DOES MAURESQUE MEAN? WELL, IT'S GENERALLY USED AS A TERM TO DEFINE A PARTICULAR STYLE OF ARCHITECTURE. FOR EXAMPLE, THE QUARTIER HABOUS NEIGHBORHOOD OF CASABLANCA FUSES MOORISH AND ART DECO INFLUENCES TO CREATE A UNIQUE STYLE...KNOWN AS MAURESQUE.

YOU KNOW WHAT? JUST MAKE THE DRINK.

1 OZ ABSINTHE

1 OZ ORGEAT

WATER

WE'D RECOMMEND A LOWBALL GLASS FOR THIS ONE.

FIRST THINGS FIRST, GO BUY SOME:

■ FINO SHERRY

OH, AND MAKE SURE YOU HAVE AN ORANGE

> TECHNICALLY, VERMOUTH IS A FORTIFIED WINE (NOT A SPIRIT). BASICALLY: WINE SPIKED WITH BRANDY.

INGREDIENTS	INSTRUCTIONS
■ 1.5 OZ FINO SHERRY	CHILL SERVING GLASS ☐
■ 1.5 OZ DRY VERMOUTH	GET MIXING GLASS ☐
■ 2 DASH ANGOSTURA BITTERS	FILL WITH ICE ☐
■ 2 DASH ORANGE BITTERS	ADD ALL INGREDIENTS ☐
■ ORANGE (GARNISH)	STIR UNTIL CHILLED ☐
	STRAIN INTO GLASS ☐
	GARNISH W/ ORANGE PEEL ☐

WHAT DO YOU THINK?

. . . .

. . . .

. . . .

DRINK THIS AGAIN?   YES ☐   NO ☐   IF DESPERATE ☐

BONUS TRIVIA

SOME TYPES OF BAMBOO CAN GROW UP TO 2" AN HOUR.

1.5 OZ
FINO SHERRY

1.5 OZ
DRY VERMOUTH

2 DASH
ORANGE BITTERS

2 DASH
ANGOSTURA
BITTERS

THIS ONE DEFINITELY CALLS FOR A MARTINI GLASS.

FIRST THINGS FIRST, GO BUY SOME:

SIMPLE SYRUP

OH, AND YOU'LL ALSO NEED AN ORANGE (AND A LEMON)

IF YOU CAN BOIL WATER, YOU CAN MAKE SIMPLE
SYRUP (OR YOU CAN JUST BE LIKE US AND BUY IT).

INGREDIENTS

INSTRUCTIONS

INGREDIENTS	INSTRUCTIONS
1 ORANGE SLICE	GET SHAKER ☐
1 LEMON SLICE	ADD FIRST 3 INGREDIENTS ☐
.75 OZ SIMPLE SYRUP	MUDDLE UNTIL MIXED ☐
3.5 OZ FINO SHERRY	FILL W/ ICE & ADD SHERRY ☐
ORANGE (GARNISH)	SHAKE UNTIL CHILLED ☐
	FILL SERVING GLASS W/ ICE ☐
	STRAIN INTO GLASS ☐
	GARNISH W/ ORANGE WEDGE ☐

WHAT DO YOU THINK?

. . . .

. . . .

DRINK THIS AGAIN?   YES ☐   NO ☐   IF DESPERATE ☐

BONUS TRIVIA

ADAM SANDLER STARRED IN THE 2014 MOVIE 'THE COBBLER.'
'SANDLER' ALSO HAPPENS TO BE DERIVED FROM 'SHOEMAKER.'

3.5 OZ
FINO
SHERRY

.75 OZ
SIMPLE
SYRUP

YOU SHOULD PROBABLY USE A HIGHBALL GLASS.

YOU PRETTY MUCH HAVE EVERYTHING YOU NEED:

LIME JUICE

OH, AND YOU'LL ALSO NEED SOME MINT

THIS DRINK IS RUMORED TO BE NAMED AFTER THE AREA
OF CHICAGO DOMINATED BY AL CAPONE & HIS MEN.

INGREDIENTS	INSTRUCTIONS
5 MINT LEAVES	GET SHAKER ☐
.75 OZ SIMPLE SYRUP	ADD FIRST 2 INGREDIENTS ☐
1 OZ LIME JUICE	MUDDLE UNTIL MIXED ☐
2 OZ DRY GIN	FILL WITH ICE ☐
MINT SPRIG (GARNISH)	SHAKE UNTIL CHILLED ☐
	STRAIN INTO GLASS ☐
	GARNISH W/ MINT SPRIG ☐

WHAT DO YOU THINK?

. . . .

. . . .

. . . .

DRINK THIS AGAIN?   YES ☐   NO ☐   IF DESPERATE ☐

BONUS TRIVIA

AL CAPONE HATED THE NICKNAME SCARFACE. CLOSE FRIENDS
ACTUALLY CALLED HIM SNORKY.

2 OZ
DRY GIN

1 OZ
LIME JUICE

.75 OZ
SIMPLE SYRUP

IF IT WERE US, WE'D USE A MARTINI GLASS.

FIRST THINGS FIRST, GO BUY SOME:

■ LEMON JUICE

AND MAKE SURE YOU HAVE AN ORANGE (AND BRANDIED CHERRIES)

PEOPLE IN THE PHILIPPINES DRINK THE MOST GIN PER CAPITA IN THE WORLD (1.4 LITERS A YEAR, ON AVERAGE).

INGREDIENTS	INSTRUCTIONS
■ 2 OZ DRY GIN	GET SHAKER ☐
■ .75 OZ SIMPLE SYRUP	ADD FIRST 3 INGREDIENTS ☐
■ .75 OZ LEMON JUICE	SHAKE UNTIL CHILLED ☐
■ CLUB SODA	GET SERVING GLASS ☐
■ ORANGE (GARNISH)	FILL WITH ICE ☐
■ BRANDIED CHERRY (GARNISH)	STRAIN INTO GLASS ☐
	TOP W/ CLUB SODA ☐
	GARNISH W/ ORANGE SLICE ☐
	ADD BRANDIED CHERRY ☐

WHAT DO YOU THINK?

. . . .

DRINK THIS AGAIN?   YES ☐   NO ☐   IF DESPERATE ☐

BONUS TRIVIA

NAMED AFTER AN 1870s PRANK WHERE PEOPLE WERE TOLD THAT
SOMEONE NAMED TOM COLLINS HAD SLANDERED THEM AT A BAR.

CLUB
SODA

2 OZ
DRY GIN

.75 OZ
LEMON JUICE

.75 OZ
SIMPLE
SYRUP

YOU SHOULD PROBABLY USE A HIGHBALL GLASS.

FIRST THINGS FIRST, GO BUY SOME:

■ MARASCHINO LIQUEUR

OH, AND HOPEFULLY YOU STILL HAVE SOME OF THAT MINT

MARASCHINO LIQUEUR IS CREATED THROUGH THE
DISTILLATION OF MARASCA CHERRIES.

INGREDIENTS	INSTRUCTIONS
■ 12 MINT LEAVES	CHILL SERVING GLASS ☐
■ 1.75 OZ DRY GIN	GET SHAKER & ADD ICE ☐
■ .5 OZ LEMON JUICE	ADD ALL INGREDIENTS ☐
■ .25 OZ SIMPLE SYRUP	SHAKE UNTIL CHILLED ☐
■ .25 OZ MARASCHINO LIQUEUR	STRAIN INTO GLASS ☐

WHAT DO YOU THINK?

. . . .

. . . .

. . . .

. . . .

DRINK THIS AGAIN?   YES ☐   NO ☐   IF DESPERATE ☐

SURE, WE'VE GOT TWO NOSTRILS...BUT THEY ONLY WORK
ONE AT A TIME WHEN WE SMELL THINGS.

.5 OZ
LEMON
JUICE

.25 OZ
SIMPLE
SYRUP

.25 OZ
MARASCHINO
LIQUEUR

1.75 OZ
DRY GIN

THIS ONE DEFINITELY CALLS FOR A MARTINI GLASS.

FIRST THINGS FIRST, GO BUY SOME:

RASPBERRY LIQUEUR

OH, AND MAKE SURE YOU HAVE EGGS AND RASPBERRIES TOO

THIS PRE-PROHIBITION COCKTAIL IS NAMED AFTER
A PHILADELPHIA MEN'S CLUB OF THE SAME NAME.

INGREDIENTS

2 OZ DRY GIN

.75 OZ EGG WHITES

.5 OZ RASPBERRY LIQUEUR

.5 OZ LEMON JUICE

3 RASPBERRIES (GARNISH)

INSTRUCTIONS

GET SHAKER ☐

ADD ALL INGREDIENTS ☐

DRY SHAKE ☐

ADD ICE & SHAKE AGAIN ☐

STRAIN INTO GLASS ☐

GARNISH W/ RASPBERRIES ☐

WHAT DO YOU THINK?

· ·

· ·

· ·

DRINK THIS AGAIN?   YES ☐   NO ☐   IF DESPERATE ☐

BONUS TRIVIA

THERE ARE APPROXIMATELY 10,000 THREE-LEAF CLOVERS
FOR EVERY 'LUCKY' FOUR-LEAF CLOVER THAT EXISTS.

2 OZ
DRY GIN

.5 OZ
LEMON
JUICE

.5 OZ
RASPBERRY
LIQUEUR

.75 OZ
EGG WHITES

USE A COUPE GLASS. TRUST US, IT'S WORTH IT.

FIRST THINGS FIRST, GO BUY SOME:

◼ CHAMPAGNE

CHECK YOUR BAR FOR ANYTHING YOU'RE GETTING LOW ON, THOUGH

THEY SAY THERE ARE 20 MILLION BUBBLES IN A BOTTLE OF CHAMPAGNE. SOUNDS LIKE A 'RAIN MAN' OUTTAKE.

INGREDIENTS

INSTRUCTIONS

- 1 OZ DRY GIN
- .5 OZ LEMON JUICE
- 2 DASH SIMPLE SYRUP
- 2 OZ CHAMPAGNE

GET SHAKER & FILL W/ ICE ☐
ADD FIRST 3 INGREDIENTS ☐
SHAKE UNTIL CHILLED ☐
POUR INTO SERVING GLASS ☐
TOP W/ CHAMPAGNE ☐

WHAT DO YOU THINK?

. . . .

. . . .

. . . .

. . . .

DRINK THIS AGAIN?   YES ☐   NO ☐   IF DESPERATE ☐

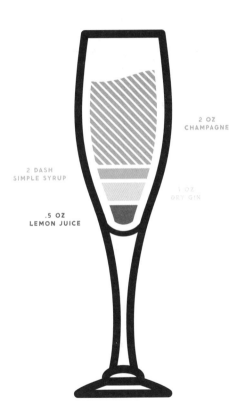

2 OZ
CHAMPAGNE

2 DASH
SIMPLE SYRUP

1 OZ
DRY GIN

.5 OZ
LEMON JUICE

FINALLY, A USE FOR THOSE CHAMPAGNE FLUTES.

YOU PRETTY MUCH HAVE EVERYTHING YOU NEED:

☐ SO MAKE A DRINK ALREADY

CHECK YOUR BAR FOR ANYTHING YOU'RE GETTING LOW ON, THOUGH

A GIMLET IS ALSO A HAND-HELD DRILL USED TO BORE
HOLES...INTO WOOD BARRELS OF GIN, FOR EXAMPLE.

INGREDIENTS   **INSTRUCTIONS**

☐ 2 OZ DRY GIN   GET SHAKER & ADD ICE ☐
☐ .75 OZ SIMPLE SYRUP   ADD ALL INGREDIENTS ☐
☐ .75 OZ LIME JUICE   SHAKE UNTIL CHILLED ☐
                              STRAIN INTO GLASS ☐

WHAT DO YOU THINK?

. . . .

. . . .

. . . .

. . . .

. . . .

DRINK THIS AGAIN?   YES ☐   NO ☐   IF DESPERATE ☐

BONUS TRIVIA

THE MOST FAMOUS GIMLET RECIPE WAS PUBLISHED IN THE
NOVEL 'THE LONG GOODBYE' BY RAYMOND CHANDLER.

.75 OZ
SIMPLE
SYRUP

2 OZ
DRY GIN

.75 OZ
LIME JUICE

THIS ONE LOOKS GREAT IN A MARTINI GLASS.

FIRST THINGS FIRST, GO BUY SOME:

▢ SUGAR CUBES

OH, AND YOU'LL ALSO NEED TO HAVE A LEMON HANDY

MARILYN MONROE ONCE BATHED IN CHAMPAGNE. IT TOOK
350 BOTTLES (AND SHE PROBABLY DIDN'T GET CLEAN).

INGREDIENTS	INSTRUCTIONS
4 OZ CHAMPAGNE	GET SERVING GLASS ▢
3 DASH ANGOSTURA BITTERS	ADD SUGAR CUBE ▢
1 SUGAR CUBE	APPLY BITTERS ▢
LEMON (GARNISH)	FILL W/ CHAMPAGNE ▢
	GARNISH W/ LEMON TWIST ▢

WHAT DO YOU THINK?

. . . .

. . . .

. . . .

. . . .

DRINK THIS AGAIN?   YES ▢   NO ▢   IF DESPERATE ▢

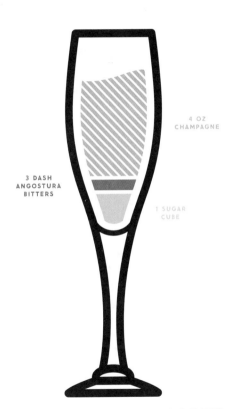

4 OZ
CHAMPAGNE

3 DASH
ANGOSTURA
BITTERS

1 SUGAR
CUBE

FINALLY, A USE FOR THOSE CHAMPAGNE FLUTES.

17

FIRST THINGS FIRST, GO BUY SOME:

☐ ORANGE JUICE (JUST GET THE NO-PULP VARIETY)

PSST: DON'T FORGET TO ADD THIS TO YOUR INVENTORY LIST

> MIMOSAS ARE A PART OF A BALANCED BREAKFAST
> (BUT THEN AGAIN, SO ARE LUCKY CHARMS).

INGREDIENTS   **INSTRUCTIONS**

☐ 3 OZ ORANGE JUICE   GET SERVING GLASS ☐
☐ 3 OZ CHAMPAGNE   ADD CHAMPAGNE ☐
                                          TOP W/ ORANGE JUICE ☐
                                                    DO NOT STIR ☐

WHAT DO YOU THINK?

. . . .

. . . .

. . . .

. . . .

. . . .

DRINK THIS AGAIN?   YES ☐   NO ☐   IF DESPERATE ☐

MAKE A MIMOSA

3 OZ
ORANGE
JUICE

3 OZ
CHAMPAGNE

CHAMPAGNE FLUTES ARE MADE FOR MIMOSAS.

FIRST THINGS FIRST, GO BUY SOME:

ABSINTHE

YOU'LL ALSO NEED SOME FRESH MINT LEAVES FOR THIS ONE

KNOWN ABSINTHE DRINKER JAMES K. POLK REPORTEDLY
ONCE DECLARED STATEHOOD FOR HIS OWN SIDEBURNS.

INGREDIENTS

1 OZ ABSINTHE
.5 OZ SIMPLE SYRUP
1 OZ CLUB SODA
8 MINT LEAVES

INSTRUCTIONS

GET SERVING GLASS ☐
ADD MINT & MUDDLE ☐
ADD FIRST 2 INGREDIENTS ☐
FILL W/ CRUSHED ICE ☐
POUR INTO A SHAKER ☐
SHAKE UNTIL CHILLED ☐
POUR BACK INTO THE GLASS ☐
TOP W/ CLUB SODA ☐

WHAT DO YOU THINK?

. . . .

. . . .

DRINK THIS AGAIN?　　YES ☐　　NO ☐　　IF DESPERATE ☐

BONUS TRIVIA

ABSINTHE, DESPITE ITS REPUTATION, HAS NEVER CONTAINED ANY SORT OF PSYCHOACTIVE SUBSTANCES. IT'S REALLY ALL JUST A MYTH. YOU KNOW WHAT REALLY CAUSED ALL OF THOSE HALLUCINATIONS? THE EXTREMELY HIGH ALCOHOL CONTENT.

PEOPLE WEREN'T HALLUCINATING...THEY WERE JUST INCREDIBLY DRUNK.

1 OZ
ABSINTHE

.5 OZ
SIMPLE
SYRUP

1 OZ
CLUB SODA

WE'D RECOMMEND A LOWBALL GLASS FOR THIS ONE.

YOU PRETTY MUCH HAVE EVERYTHING YOU NEED:

■ SO MAKE A DRINK ALREADY

CHECK YOUR BAR FOR ANYTHING YOU'RE GETTING LOW ON, THOUGH

> ONLY 1 OUT OF EVERY 9,000 MEN KNOW HOW TO TIE
> A BOW TIE. 97% OF THEM ARE LIKELY HIPSTERS.

INGREDIENTS   INSTRUCTIONS

■ 2 OZ DRY GIN   CHILL SERVING GLASS ☐
▨ 1 OZ FINO SHERRY   GET A MIXING GLASS ☐
■ 1 DASH ORANGE BITTERS   FILL WITH ICE ☐
                              ADD ALL INGREDIENTS ☐
                                STIR UNTIL CHILLED ☐
                                STRAIN INTO GLASS ☐

WHAT DO YOU THINK?

. . . .

. . . .

. . . .

DRINK THIS AGAIN?   YES ☐   NO ☐   IF DESPERATE ☐

BONUS TRIVIA

THE TUXEDO IS NAMED AFTER THE RESORT VILLAGE OF TUXEDO PARK, NY. THERE, DURING THE 1880s, YOUNG MEN FIRST BEGAN WEARING DINNER JACKETS WITHOUT TAILS. THOSE REBELS.

1 OZ
FINO
SHERRY

2 OZ
DRY GIN

1 DASH
ORANGE
BITTERS

IF IT WERE US, WE'D USE A COUPE GLASS.

FIRST THINGS FIRST, GO BUY SOME:

☐ GRENADINE

DON'T FORGET TO ADD THIS TO YOUR INVENTORY LIST

THE BARTENDER THAT DEVELOPED THIS DRINK ALSO
CREATED THE BLOODY MARY & THE FRENCH 75.

INGREDIENTS   INSTRUCTIONS

1.5 OZ DRY GIN   CHILL SERVING GLASS ☐
1.5 OZ ORANGE JUICE   GET SHAKER & ADD ICE ☐
1 TSP ABSINTHE   ADD ALL INGREDIENTS ☐
1 TSP SIMPLE SYRUP   SHAKE UNTIL CHILLED ☐
1 TSP GRENADINE   STRAIN INTO GLASS ☐

WHAT DO YOU THINK?

. . . .

. . . .

. . . .

. . . .

DRINK THIS AGAIN?   YES ☐   NO ☐   IF DESPERATE ☐

BONUS TRIVIA

NAMED AFTER THE 1920s EXPERIMENTS OF SERGE VORONOFF,
WHO GRAFTED MONKEY GLANDS TO HUMAN TESTICLES.

1.5 OZ
DRY GIN

1.5 OZ
ORANGE
JUICE

1 TSP
ABSINTHE

1 TSP
GRENADINE

1 TSP
SIMPLE
SYRUP

THIS ONE DEFINITELY CALLS FOR A MARTINI GLASS.

FIRST THINGS FIRST, GO BUY SOME:

CREAM

OH, AND YOU'LL ALSO NEED AN EGG (AND SOME NUTMEG)

IT'S NOT JUST PLAYING CARDS. DICE THAT LAND WITH A SINGLE PIP FACE UP ARE KNOWN AS ACES AS WELL.

INGREDIENTS

1 OZ DRY GIN	
.5 OZ GRENADINE	
.5 OZ CREAM	
1 EGG WHITE	
.25 OZ LEMON JUICE	
GRATED NUTMEG (GARNISH)	

INSTRUCTIONS

GET SHAKER & FILL W/ ICE ☐
ADD ALL INGREDIENTS ☐
SHAKE UNTIL CHILLED ☐
STRAIN INTO SERVING GLASS ☐
GARNISH W/ NUTMEG ☐

WHAT DO YOU THINK?

. . . .

. . . .

. . . .

DRINK THIS AGAIN?   YES ☐   NO ☐   IF DESPERATE ☐

BONUS TRIVIA

WHEN TOM SHADYAC, THE DIRECTOR OF 'ACE VENTURA: PET DETECTIVE,' FIRST SAW THE FINAL FILM, HE WAS WORRIED THAT IT WOULD END HIS (AND JIM CARREY'S) CAREER.

1 OZ
DRY GIN

1 EGG
WHITE

.5 OZ
GRENADINE

.5 OZ
CREAM

.25 OZ
LEMON JUICE

USE A COUPE GLASS. TRUST US, IT'S WORTH IT.

YOU PRETTY MUCH HAVE EVERYTHING YOU NEED:

▪ THIS BOOK IS PAYING OFF ALREADY, ISN'T IT?

CHECK YOUR BAR FOR ANYTHING YOU'RE GETTING LOW ON, THOUGH

THIS DRINK WAS CREATED BY ERNEST HEMINGWAY, AND NAMED AFTER HIS 1932 BOOK ABOUT BULLFIGHTING.

INGREDIENTS	INSTRUCTIONS
▪ 1.5 OZ ABSINTHE	ADD ABSINTHE TO GLASS ☐
▪ CHAMPAGNE	SLOWLY TOP W/ CHAMPAGNE ☐

WHAT DO YOU THINK?

· ·

· ·

· ·

· ·

· ·

· ·

DRINK THIS AGAIN? YES ☐ NO ☐ IF DESPERATE ☐

HEMINGWAY'S RECIPE: 'POUR ONE JIGGER ABSINTHE INTO A CHAMPAGNE GLASS. ADD ICED CHAMPAGNE UNTIL IT ATTAINS THE PROPER OPALESCENT MILKINESS. DRINK 3-5 OF THESE SLOWLY.'

CHAMP-
AGNE

1.5 OZ
ABSINTHE

SCREW HEMINGWAY, IT'S BETTER IN A COUPE GLASS.

MAKE A BUNNY HUG

FIRST THINGS FIRST, GO BUY SOME:

▨ TENNESSEE WHISKEY

DON'T FORGET TO ADD THIS TO YOUR INVENTORY LIST

NAMED AFTER A DANCE THAT WAS THE EARLY 1900s
EQUIVALENT OF DIRTY DANCING. THEY TOUCHED. *GASP*

INGREDIENTS

INSTRUCTIONS

■ 1 OZ DRY GIN
▨ 1 OZ TENNESSEE WHISKEY
▨ 1 OZ ABSINTHE

GET SHAKER & ADD ICE ☐
ADD INGREDIENTS ☐
SHAKE UNTIL CHILLED ☐
POUR INTO SERVING GLASS ☐

WHAT DO YOU THINK?

. . . .

. . . .

. . . .

. . . .

. . . .

DRINK THIS AGAIN? YES ☐ NO ☐ IF DESPERATE ☐

BONUS TRIVIA

RABBITS ARE PHYSICALLY INCAPABLE OF THROWING UP.

1 OZ
DRY GIN

1 OZ
TENNESSEE
WHISKEY

1 OZ
ABSINTHE

THIS ONE CALLS FOR A MARTINI GLASS.

FIRST THINGS FIRST, GO BUY SOME:

GENEVER GIN (TRY OUR FAVORITE: BOLS GENEVER)

TOTALLY NOT AN AD (BUT THEY ARE WELCOME TO SEND US SOME)*

SURE, YOU ALREADY HAVE A GIN...BUT GENEVERS ARE
WAY DIFFERENT (AND WAY BETTER IN OUR OPINION).

INGREDIENTS

INSTRUCTIONS

4 DASH ANGOSTURA BITTERS — GET SERVING GLASS ☐

3 OZ GENEVER GIN — ADD ICE & BITTERS ☐

1 TBSP LIME JUICE — STIR UNTIL COMBINED ☐

1 TBSP SIMPLE SYRUP — ADD OTHER INGREDIENTS ☐

STIR AGAIN ☐

WHAT DO YOU THINK?

. . . .

. . . .

. . . .

*JUST IN CASE: BRASS MONKEY 1107 HICKORY ST. KANSAS CITY, MO 64101

DRINK THIS AGAIN?   YES ☐   NO ☐   IF DESPERATE ☐

BONUS TRIVIA

ERNEST HEMINGWAY (THE CREATOR OF THIS DRINK) DESCRIBED
IT AS A COCKTAIL TO BE ENJOYED FROM 11:00 AM ON.

3 OZ
GENEVER
GIN

4 DASH
ANGOSTURA
BITTERS

1 TBSP
SIMPLE
SYRUP

1 TBSP
LIME
JUICE

YOU SHOULD PROBABLY USE A HIGHBALL GLASS.

FIRST THINGS FIRST, GO BUY SOME:

TABASCO SAUCE

OH, AND MAKE SURE YOU HAVE AN EGG TOO

THIS COCKTAIL GETS ITS NAME FROM THE RAW EGG
INSIDE. THAT'S THE MOON, GET IT?

INGREDIENTS   **INSTRUCTIONS**

3 OZ TENNESSEE WHISKEY   GET SERVING GLASS ☐
1 RAW EGG   CRACK THE EGG INSIDE ☐
TABASCO SAUCE   LEAVE YOLK UNBROKEN ☐
                                 GENTLY POUR IN WHISKEY ☐
                                   ADD TABASCO TO TASTE ☐

WHAT DO YOU THINK?

. . . .

. . . .

. . . .

. . . .

DRINK THIS AGAIN?   YES ☐   NO ☐   IF DESPERATE ☐

BONUS TRIVIA

WHILE KNOWN AS A HANGOVER CURE, IT ALSO CONTAINS
ALCOHOL. SO IT'S MORE LIKE A HANGOVER DELAYER.

3 OZ
TENNESSEE
WHISKEY

1 RAW
EGG

TABASCO
SAUCE

THIS ONE LOOKS GREAT IN A HIGHBALL GLASS.

YOU PRETTY MUCH HAVE EVERYTHING YOU NEED:

■ SO WATCH SOME 'MAD MEN' TO GET IN THE MOOD

JUST MAKE SURE THAT YOU HAVE AN ORANGE LAYING AROUND

SAID TO BE A FAVORITE DRINK OF GEORGE LUCAS, THEY PROBABLY HELP HIM SLEEP ON HIS PILES OF MONEY.

INGREDIENTS

INSTRUCTIONS

INGREDIENTS	INSTRUCTIONS
■ 2 OZ TENNESSEE WHISKEY	GET SERVING GLASS ☐
■ 2 DASH ANGOSTURA BITTERS	ADD SUGAR & BITTERS ☐
▨ 1 SUGAR CUBE	MUDDLE UNTIL MIXED ☐
■ ORANGE (GARNISH)	ADD A LARGE ICE CUBE ☐
	POUR IN WHISKEY ☐
	GARNISH W/ ORANGE TWIST ☐

WHAT DO YOU THINK?

. . . .

. . . .

. . . .

DRINK THIS AGAIN?   YES ☐   NO ☐   IF DESPERATE ☐

BONUS TRIVIA

IN A 2016 SURVEY OF BARTENDERS AT THE TOP 100 BARS IN THE COUNTRY, THE OLD FASHIONED WAS DETERMINED TO BE THE MOST POPULAR DRINK ORDER AMONG BAR-GOERS.

SO IT'S EITHER A REALLY GOOD DRINK OR A REALLY EASY NAME TO REMEMBER.

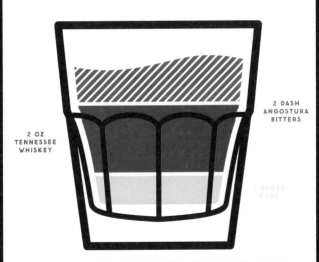

2 DASH ANGOSTURA BITTERS

2 OZ TENNESSEE WHISKEY

1 SUGAR CUBE

IT'S ONLY PROPER TO SERVE THIS IN A LOWBALL GLASS.

FIRST THINGS FIRST, GO BUY SOME:

SWEET VERMOUTH

OH, AND YOU'LL ALSO NEED SOME ORANGES (AND PINEAPPLE)

POLLYANNA MEANS AN EXCESSIVELY CHEERFUL OR
OPTIMISTIC PERSON. SO BASICALLY, NOT US.

INGREDIENTS	INSTRUCTIONS
3 SLICES PINEAPPLE	GET SHAKER ☐
3 SLICES ORANGE	ADD FIRST 2 INGREDIENTS ☐
1 SPLASH GRENADINE	MUDDLE UNTIL MIXED ☐
.5 OZ SWEET VERMOUTH	FILL WITH ICE ☐
2 OZ DRY GIN	ADD OTHER INGREDIENTS ☐
PINEAPPLE (GARNISH)	SHAKE UNTIL CHILLED ☐
	STRAIN INTO GLASS ☐
	GARNISH W/ PINEAPPLE WEDGE ☐

WHAT DO YOU THINK?

. . . .

. . . .

DRINK THIS AGAIN?   YES ☐   NO ☐   IF DESPERATE ☐

BONUS TRIVIA

HAYLEY MILLS PLAYED THE TITLE CHARACTER OF POLLYANNA
IN THE 1960 FILM THAT YOU LIKELY DIDN'T KNOW EXISTED.

2 OZ
DRY GIN

1 SPLASH
GRENADINE

.5 OZ SWEET
VERMOUTH

IF IT WERE US, WE'D USE A MARTINI GLASS.

FIRST THINGS FIRST, GO BUY SOME:

■ OLD TOM GIN

CHECK YOUR BAR FOR ANYTHING YOU'RE GETTING LOW ON, THOUGH

WE REALLY WISH THIS TYPE OF GIN WAS NAMED AFTER
AN OLD GUY NAMED TOM, BUT THE INTERNET SAYS NO.

INGREDIENTS

INSTRUCTIONS

■ 1.5 OZ OLD TOM GIN
■ 1.5 OZ SWEET VERMOUTH
■ 1.25 OZ MARASCHINO LIQUEUR
■ 2 DASH ANGOSTURA BITTERS

CHILL SERVING GLASS ☐
GET MIXING GLASS ☐
FILL WITH ICE ☐
ADD INGREDIENTS ☐
STIR UNTIL CHILLED ☐
STRAIN INTO SERVING GLASS ☐

WHAT DO YOU THINK?

. . . .

. . . .

. . . .

DRINK THIS AGAIN?   YES ☐   NO ☐   IF DESPERATE ☐

BONUS TRIVIA

THIS DRINK DATES BACK TO THE 1860s, AND IS THOUGHT TO
BE THE FATHER OF THE MARTINI. LIKE, IT INSPIRED IT. IT
DIDN'T IMPREGNATE A COSMOPOLITAN.

1.5 OZ
OLD TOM
GIN

2 DASH
ANGOSTURA
BITTERS

1.25 OZ
MARASCHINO
LIQUEUR

1.5 OZ SWEET
VERMOUTH

USE A COUPE GLASS. TRUST US, IT'S WORTH IT.

FIRST THINGS FIRST, GO BUY SOME:

HONEY (THE BOTTLE CAN EVEN BE SHAPED LIKE A BEAR)

OH, AND MAKE SURE YOU HAVE AN ORANGE TOO.

ITS NAME COMES FROM THE (CURRENT AT THE TIME)
PROHIBITION-ERA SLANG PHRASE MEANING 'THE BEST.'

INGREDIENTS

INSTRUCTIONS

1.5 OZ DRY GIN

2 TSP HONEY

.5 OZ LEMON JUICE

.5 OZ ORANGE JUICE

ORANGE (GARNISH)

GET SHAKER ☐

ADD FIRST 2 INGREDIENTS ☐

STIR UNTIL DISSOLVED ☐

ADD ALL JUICES ☐

FILL WITH ICE ☐

SHAKE UNTIL CHILLED ☐

STRAIN INTO SERVING GLASS ☐

GARNISH W/ ORANGE TWIST ☐

WHAT DO YOU THINK?

. . . .

. . . .

DRINK THIS AGAIN?   YES ☐   NO ☐   IF DESPERATE ☐

BONUS TRIVIA

AMERICANS IN THE 1920s LOVED ODD PHRASES. THEY ALSO CAME
UP WITH 'THE SNAKE'S HIPS', 'THE SARDINE'S WHISKERS', AND
'THE CAT'S PAJAMAS'...ALL MEANING THE EXACT SAME THING.

1.5 OZ
DRY GIN

2 TSP
HONEY

.5 OZ
LEMON
JUICE

.5 OZ
ORANGE
JUICE

A COUPE GLASS IS DEFINITELY YOUR BEST BET.

YOU PRETTY MUCH HAVE EVERYTHING YOU NEED:

JUST MAKE SURE YOU STILL HAVE ORANGE JUICE

OH, AND YOU'LL ALSO NEED AN ORANGE

INVENTED DURING PROHIBITION IN AN ATTEMPT TO
MASK THE HORRIBLE TASTE OF 'BATHTUB GIN.'

INGREDIENTS

INSTRUCTIONS

1.5 OZ DRY GIN

1.5 OZ SWEET VERMOUTH

1.5 OZ ORANGE JUICE

ORANGE (GARNISH)

GET SHAKER & ADD ICE ☐

ADD ALL INGREDIENTS ☐

SHAKE UNTIL CHILLED ☐

STRAIN INTO GLASS ☐

GARNISH W/ ORANGE SLICE ☐

WHAT DO YOU THINK?

. . . .

. . . .

. . . .

. . . .

DRINK THIS AGAIN?   YES ☐   NO ☐   IF DESPERATE ☐

BONUS TRIVIA

ESSENTIALLY, A FANCY PREQUEL TO SNOOP DOGG'S 1994 HIT.

1.5 OZ
DRY GIN

1.5 OZ
SWEET
VERMOUTH

1.5 OZ
ORANGE
JUICE

THIS ONE LOOKS GREAT IN A MARTINI GLASS.

FIRST THINGS FIRST, GO BUY SOME:

GINGER ALE

YOU'LL ALSO NEED A LEMON TO GARNISH THIS ONE

HOW DID THIS DRINK GET ITS NAME? WE HAVE NO IDEA.
A SURVEY OF ONE PRESBYTERIAN DIDN'T KNOW EITHER.

INGREDIENTS **INSTRUCTIONS**

1.5 OZ TENNESSEE WHISKEY GET SERVING GLASS ☐
2 OZ CLUB SODA FILL WITH ICE ☐
2 OZ GINGER ALE POUR IN WHISKEY ☐
LEMON (GARNISH) ADD OTHER INGREDIENTS ☐
STIR UNTIL CHILLED ☐
GARNISH W/ LEMON WEDGE ☐

WHAT DO YOU THINK?

. . . .

. . . .

. . . .

. . . .

DRINK THIS AGAIN? YES ☐ NO ☐ IF DESPERATE ☐

BONUS TRIVIA

GOOD NEWS: THE PRESBYTERIAN CHURCH DOESN'T CONSIDER DRINKING MODERATE AMOUNTS OF ALCOHOL TO BE A SIN.

2 OZ
CLUB SODA

1.5 OZ
TENNESSEE
WHISKEY

2 OZ
GINGER ALE

YOU SHOULD PROBABLY USE A HIGHBALL GLASS.

FIRST THINGS FIRST, GO BUY SOME:

VODKA (JUST DON'T GET A FLAVORED ONE)

OH, AND MAKE SURE YOU HAVE AN ORANGE AROUND

THIS WAS (SUPPOSEDLY) A FAVORITE DRINK
OF WRITER TRUMAN CAPOTE.

INGREDIENTS

INSTRUCTIONS

4 OZ ORANGE JUICE
2 OZ VODKA
ORANGE (GARNISH)

GET SERVING GLASS ☐
FILL WITH ICE ☐
ADD ALL INGREDIENTS ☐
STIR UNTIL CHILLED ☐
GARNISH W/ ORANGE SLICE ☐

WHAT DO YOU THINK?

. . . .

. . . .

. . . .

DRINK THIS AGAIN? YES ☐ NO ☐ IF DESPERATE ☐

BONUS TRIVIA

ONE ORIGIN STORY CLAIMS THAT OIL WORKERS WOULD SECRETLY
ADD VODKA TO THEIR OJ...AND STIR IT WITH A SCREWDRIVER.

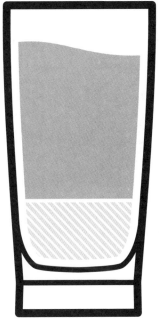

4 OZ
ORANGE
JUICE

2 OZ
VODKA

WE'D SUGGEST A HIGHBALL FOR THIS ONE.

FIRST THINGS FIRST, GO BUY SOME:

▮ TRIPLE SEC

CHECK YOUR BAR FOR ANYTHING YOU'RE GETTING LOW ON, THOUGH

> THE WORLD RECORD FOR THE MOST TANGO SPINS IN
> A MINUTE IS 37. NO WORD ON NON-TANGO SPINS.

INGREDIENTS

INSTRUCTIONS

▨ 1 OZ DRY GIN   GET SHAKER & FILL W/ ICE ☐

▮ .5 OZ DRY VERMOUTH   ADD ALL INGREDIENTS ☐

▨ .5 OZ SWEET VERMOUTH   SHAKE UNTIL CHILLED ☐

▮ .5 TSP TRIPLE SEC   STRAIN INTO GLASS ☐

▨ 1 TBSP ORANGE JUICE

WHAT DO YOU THINK?

. . . .

. . . .

. . . .

. . . .

DRINK THIS AGAIN?   YES ☐   NO ☐   IF DESPERATE ☐

BONUS TRIVIA

'TANGO & CASH' HIT THEATERS ON DECEMBER 22, 1989,
MAKING IT THE LAST FILM TO BE RELEASED IN THE 1980s.

.5 OZ DRY
VERMOUTH

1 OZ
DRY GIN

.5 OZ
SWEET
VERMOUTH

1 TBSP
ORANGE
JUICE

.5 TSP
TRIPLE
SEC

WE'D USE A MARTINI GLASS, BUT IT'S YOUR LIFE.

YOU PRETTY MUCH HAVE EVERYTHING YOU NEED:

■ JUST CHECK TO SEE IF YOU STILL HAVE GINGER ALE

OH, AND YOU'LL NEED A LIME OR TWO

COPPER DOORKNOBS ARE SELF-DISINFECTING, SO BEAT
THE RUSH AND GET READY FOR THE NEXT PANDEMIC.

INGREDIENTS   INSTRUCTIONS

■ 2 OZ VODKA   GET SHAKER & FILL W/ ICE ☐
■ 5 OZ GINGER ALE   ADD ALL INGREDIENTS ☐
■ LIME (GARNISH)   SHAKE UNTIL CHILLED ☐
                        GET SERVING GLASS & ADD ICE ☐
                                STRAIN INTO GLASS ☐
                            SQUEEZE IN LIME WEDGE ☐
                                       DROP IT IN ☐

WHAT DO YOU THINK?

. . . .

. . . .

DRINK THIS AGAIN?   YES ☐   NO ☐   IF DESPERATE ☐

AN ENZYME IN THE VENOM OF COPPERHEAD SNAKES HAS BEEN
SHOWN TO INHIBIT THE GROWTH OF CANCER CELLS.

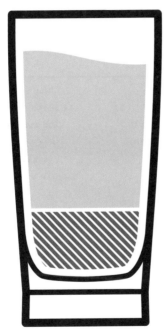

5 OZ
GINGER ALE

2 OZ
VODKA

THIS ONE CALLS FOR A HIGHBALL GLASS.

FIRST THINGS FIRST, GO BUY SOME:

■ LILLET BLANC

OH, AND MAKE SURE YOU HAVE A LEMON TOO

> OKAY, THE ORIGINAL RECIPE CALLED FOR KINA LILLET,
> JUST IN CASE YOU'RE SOME KIND OF COCKTAIL SNOB.

INGREDIENTS

INSTRUCTIONS

- 2 OZ DRY GIN
- .5 OZ VODKA
- .5 OZ LILLET BLANC
- LEMON (GARNISH)

CHILL SERVING GLASS ☐
GET SHAKER & FILL W/ ICE ☐
ADD ALL INGREDIENTS ☐
SHAKE UNTIL CHILLED ☐
STRAIN INTO GLASS ☐
GARNISH W/ LEMON TWIST ☐

WHAT DO YOU THINK?

. . . .

. . . .

. . . .

DRINK THIS AGAIN? YES ☐ NO ☐ IF DESPERATE ☐

THIS DRINK MADE ITS DEBUT IN THE 1953 JAMES BOND NOVEL 'CASINO ROYALE.' IT WAS CREATED BY THE AUTHOR, IAN FLEMING, AND NAMED AFTER THE FICTIONAL DOUBLE AGENT VESPER LYND.

2 OZ
DRY GIN

.5 OZ
VODKA

.5 OZ
LILLET BLANC

USE A COUPE GLASS. TRUST US, IT'S WORTH IT.

FIRST THINGS FIRST, GO BUY SOME:

▢ GALLIANO

PSST: YOU'LL ALSO NEED AN ORANGE FOR THIS ONE

SPOILER ALERT: GALLIANO IS A SWEET HERBAL
LIQUEUR WITH ITS OWN DISTINCT VANILLA FLAVOR.

INGREDIENTS

- 1.5 OZ VODKA
- 4 OZ ORANGE JUICE
- .5 OZ GALLIANO
- ORANGE (GARNISH)

INSTRUCTIONS

GET SERVING GLASS ▢
FILL WITH ICE ▢
ADD FIRST 2 INGREDIENTS ▢
STIR UNTIL CHILLED ▢
FLOAT* GALLIANO ON TOP ▢
GARNISH W/ ORANGE SLICE ▢

WHAT DO YOU THINK?

. . . .

. . . .

. . . .

*IF YOU DON'T KNOW HOW, CHECK OUT DRINK 52.

DRINK THIS AGAIN?   YES ▢   NO ▢   IF DESPERATE ▢

BONUS TRIVIA

IN CB LINGO, A HARVEY WALLBANGER REFERS TO A DRUNK DRIVER THAT IS DRIFTING BACK AND FORTH ACROSS THE ROAD.

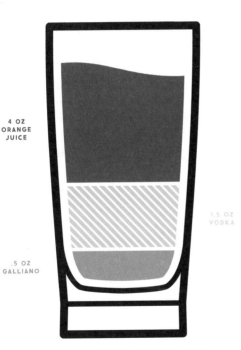

4 OZ
ORANGE
JUICE

1.5 OZ
VODKA

.5 OZ
GALLIANO

WE'D RECOMMEND A HIGHBALL GLASS.

FIRST THINGS FIRST, GO BUY SOME:

☐ DARK RUM

AND MAYBE CHECK THE EXPIRATION DATE ON THAT CREAM

THIS DRINK REGAINED A BIT OF POPULARITY AFTER THE
1980 RELEASE OF THE MOVIE 'THE BLUES BROTHERS.'

INGREDIENTS

INSTRUCTIONS

4 OZ ORANGE JUICE	GET A MIXING GLASS ☐
1 OZ DARK RUM	PULL OUT THE HAND BLENDER ☐
1 OZ VODKA	ADD ALL INGREDIENTS ☐
1 OZ CREAM	BLEND BRIEFLY ☐
	GET SERVING GLASS & ADD ICE ☐
	POUR IN MIXTURE ☐
	STIR TO COMBINE ☐

WHAT DO YOU THINK?

. . . .

. . . .

DRINK THIS AGAIN?   YES ☐   NO ☐   IF DESPERATE ☐

BONUS TRIVIA

BECAUSE OF THEIR HIGH RESISTANCE TO PLANT DISEASES, ORANGES ARE MORE LIKELY TO BE KILLED BY LIGHTNING.

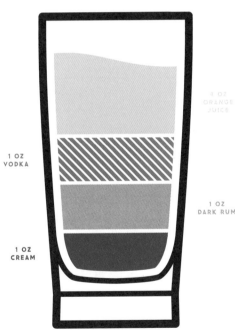

1 OZ
ORANGE
JUICE

1 OZ
VODKA

1 OZ
DARK RUM

1 OZ
CREAM

WE'D SUGGEST A HIGHBALL, BUT DO WHAT YOU WANT.

FIRST THINGS FIRST, GO BUY SOME:

▮ WHITE RUM

OH, AND YOU'LL ALSO NEED TO HAVE AN EXTRA LEMON

A FAVORITE (AND NAMESAKE) OF THE 1930s ACTRESS BEST KNOWN AS THE FIRST 'BLONDE BOMBSHELL.'

INGREDIENTS

INSTRUCTIONS

▮ 2 OZ WHITE RUM

▮ 2 OZ SWEET VERMOUTH

▮ LEMON (GARNISH)

GET SHAKER & ADD ICE ☐

ADD ALL INGREDIENTS ☐

SHAKE UNTIL CHILLED ☐

STRAIN INTO SERVING GLASS ☐

GARNISH W/ LEMON TWIST ☐

WHAT DO YOU THINK?

. . . .

. . . .

. . . .

. . . .

DRINK THIS AGAIN?   YES ☐   NO ☐   IF DESPERATE ☐

BONUS TRIVIA

JEAN HARLOW WAS BORN IN KANSAS CITY. SO WAS THIS BOOK.

2 OZ
WHITE RUM

2 OZ
SWEET
VERMOUTH

THIS ONE DEFINITELY CALLS FOR A MARTINI GLASS.

YOU PRETTY MUCH HAVE EVERYTHING YOU NEED:

JUST MAKE SURE YOU STILL HAVE ENOUGH

OH, AND YOU'LL ALSO NEED A LIME

DESPITE POPULAR BELIEF, GINGER IS ACTUALLY A
RHIZOME (AN UNDERGROUND STEM), NOT A ROOT.

INGREDIENTS

INSTRUCTIONS

2 OZ DARK RUM — GET SERVING GLASS ☐

2 DASH ANGOSTURA BITTERS — FILL WITH ICE ☐

GINGER ALE — ADD FIRST INGREDIENT ☐

LIME (GARNISH) — TOP W/ BITTERS & GINGER ALE ☐

STIR UNTIL COMBINED ☐

GARNISH W/ LIME WEDGE ☐

WHAT DO YOU THINK?

. . . .

. . . .

. . . .

DRINK THIS AGAIN?   YES ☐   NO ☐   IF DESPERATE ☐

BONUS TRIVIA

TINA LOUISE (GINGER) IS THE LAST SURVIVING CAST MEMBER
OF 'GILLIGAN'S ISLAND.' SORRY ABOUT THE JINX, TINA.

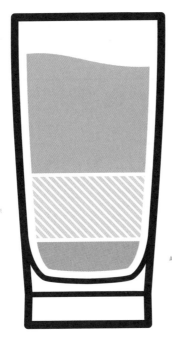

GINGER
ALE

2 OZ
DARK RUM

2 DASH
ANGOSTURA
BITTERS

TRY IT IN A HIGHBALL GLASS (OR A COPPER MUG).

YOU PRETTY MUCH HAVE EVERYTHING YOU NEED:

▪ JUST MAKE SURE YOU HAVE LIMES

CHECK YOUR BAR FOR ANYTHING YOU'RE GETTING LOW ON, THOUGH

INITIALLY CREATED BY ROBERT LOUIS STEVENSON'S DOCTOR, BERNHARD FUNK. IT EVOLVED LATER THOUGH.

INGREDIENTS

- 1.5 OZ WHITE RUM
- 1 TSP ABSINTHE
- .75 OZ LIME JUICE
- .5 OZ GRENADINE
- 1 OZ CLUB SODA
- LIME (GARNISH)

INSTRUCTIONS

GET SHAKER & FILL W/ ICE ☐
ADD FIRST 4 INGREDIENTS ☐
SHAKE UNTIL CHILLED ☐
ADD CLUB SODA & STIR ☐
GET SERVING GLASS & ADD ICE ☐
STRAIN INTO GLASS ☐
GARNISH W/ LIME WEDGE ☐

WHAT DO YOU THINK?

. . . .

. . . .

DRINK THIS AGAIN?   YES ☐   NO ☐   IF DESPERATE ☐

BONUS TRIVIA

'FUNK' WAS ONCE DEFINED IN DICTIONARIES AS THE SMELL
OF SEXUAL INTERCOURSE. YOU'RE WELCOME.

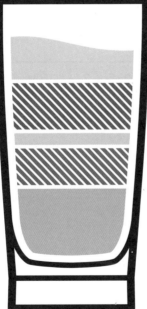

.75 OZ
LIME JUICE

1 OZ
CLUB SODA

1 TSP
ABSINTHE

.5 OZ
GRENADINE

1.5 OZ
WHITE RUM

YOU SHOULD PROBABLY USE A HIGHBALL GLASS.

FIRST THINGS FIRST, GO BUY SOME:

GRAPEFRUIT JUICE

OH, AND MAKE SURE YOU HAVE SOME SUGAR

THE LAST FRIDAY OF OCTOBER IS NEVADA DAY, A LEGAL
HOLIDAY IN NEVADA. IN OTHER STATES? NOT SO MUCH.

INGREDIENTS	INSTRUCTIONS
2 OZ WHITE RUM	CHILL SERVING GLASS ☐
2 OZ GRAPEFRUIT JUICE	GET SHAKER ☐
1 DASH ANGOSTURA BITTERS	FILL WITH ICE ☐
2 TSP SUGAR	ADD ALL INGREDIENTS ☐
1 OZ LIME JUICE	SHAKE UNTIL COMBINED ☐
	STRAIN INTO GLASS ☐

WHAT DO YOU THINK?

. . . .

. . . .

. . . .

DRINK THIS AGAIN?   YES ☐   NO ☐   IF DESPERATE ☐

BONUS TRIVIA

LAS VEGAS, NEVADA, HAS MORE HOTEL ROOMS THAN ANY
OTHER CITY ON EARTH. LEAVE THAT BLACK LIGHT AT HOME.

1 OZ
LIME JUICE

2 OZ
GRAPEFRUIT
JUICE

2 OZ
WHITE RUM

2 TSP
SUGAR

1 DASH
ANGOSTURA
BITTERS

THIS ONE LOOKS GREAT IN A MARTINI GLASS.

YOU PRETTY MUCH HAVE EVERYTHING YOU NEED:

☐ JUST MAKE SURE YOU STILL HAVE FRESH ORANGE JUICE

OH, AND YOU'LL ALSO NEED SUGAR (AND AN ORANGE)

PRESIDENT ROOSEVELT WAS AN AVID BOXER WHILE IN THE WHITE HOUSE (UNTIL HE SWITCHED TO JIU-JITSU).

INGREDIENTS

- 1.75 OZ DARK RUM
- .5 OZ DRY VERMOUTH
- .25 OZ ORANGE JUICE
- .25 TSP SUGAR
- ORANGE (GARNISH)

INSTRUCTIONS

- GET SHAKER & FILL W/ ICE ☐
- ADD ALL INGREDIENTS ☐
- SHAKE UNTIL CHILLED ☐
- STRAIN INTO SERVING GLASS ☐
- GARNISH W/ ORANGE TWIST ☐

WHAT DO YOU THINK?

. . . .

. . . .

. . . .

DRINK THIS AGAIN?   YES ☐   NO ☐   IF DESPERATE ☐

BONUS TRIVIA

ROOSEVELT ALSO HAD AN EXCEPTIONAL MEMORY. IN SEVERAL
DOCUMENTED CASES, HE WAS ABLE TO RECITE OBSCURE POETRY
AND OTHER PASSAGES OVER A DECADE AFTER HE READ THEM.

1.75 OZ
DARK
RUM

.25 TSP
SUGAR

.25 OZ
ORANGE
JUICE

.5 OZ DRY
VERMOUTH

USE A COUPE GLASS. TRUST US, IT'S WORTH IT.

YOU PRETTY MUCH HAVE EVERYTHING YOU NEED:

JUST MAKE SURE YOU HAVE MINT

MAYBE CHECK ON THE FRESHNESS OF THAT CLUB SODA TOO

THE ROMANS BELIEVED THAT EATING MINT WOULD
INCREASE INTELLIGENCE.

INGREDIENTS   **INSTRUCTIONS**

3 MINT LEAVES   GET SHAKER ☐
.5 OZ SIMPLE SYRUP   ADD FIRST 2 INGREDIENTS ☐
2 OZ WHITE RUM   MUDDLE & FILL W/ ICE ☐
.75 OZ LIME JUICE   ADD RUM & LIME JUICE ☐
CLUB SODA   SHAKE UNTIL CHILLED ☐
MINT SPRIG (GARNISH)   FILL GLASS W/ ICE ☐
                                               STRAIN INTO GLASS ☐
                                              TOP WITH CLUB SODA ☐
                                           GARNISH W/ MINT SPRIG ☐

WHAT DO YOU THINK?

. . . .

DRINK THIS AGAIN?   YES ☐   NO ☐   IF DESPERATE ☐

THE NAME MOJITO COMES FROM THE WORD 'MOJO,' MEANING
TALISMAN OR MAGIC CHARM.

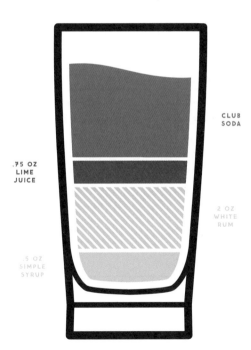

CLUB
SODA

.75 OZ
LIME
JUICE

2 OZ
WHITE
RUM

.5 OZ
SIMPLE
SYRUP

YOU SHOULD DEFINITELY USE A HIGHBALL GLASS.

FIRST THINGS FIRST, GO BUY SOME:

■ BLANCO TEQUILA

OH, YOU'LL ALSO NEED SALT, CUCUMBER, & LIMES FOR THIS ONE

BLANCO TEQUILA IS UNAGED, WHICH ALLOWS FOR
STRONGER NOTES OF AGAVE TO COME THROUGH.

INGREDIENTS	INSTRUCTIONS
2 OZ BLANCO TEQUILA	GET SERVING GLASS ☐
.75 OZ SIMPLE SYRUP	RIM W/ LIME & DIP IN SALT ☐
1 DASH TABASCO SAUCE	GET SHAKER ☐
5 CUCUMBER SLICES	ADD ALL INGREDIENTS ☐
3 LIME WEDGES	MUDDLE UNTIL MIXED ☐
SALT (RIM OF GLASS)	ADD ICE & SHAKE HARD ☐
LIME (GARNISH)	FILL SERVING GLASS W/ ICE ☐
	STRAIN INTO GLASS ☐
	GARNISH W/ LIME WEDGE ☐

WHAT DO YOU THINK?

....

DRINK THIS AGAIN?   YES ☐   NO ☐   IF DESPERATE ☐

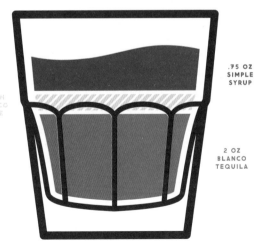

1 DASH
TABASCO
SAUCE

.75 OZ
SIMPLE
SYRUP

2 OZ
BLANCO
TEQUILA

WE'D RECOMMEND A LOWBALL GLASS FOR THIS ONE.

YOU PRETTY MUCH HAVE EVERYTHING YOU NEED:

☐ JUST MAKE SURE THAT YOU HAVE A LIME

CHECK YOUR BAR FOR ANYTHING YOU'RE GETTING LOW ON, THOUGH

RUMORED TO BE ONE OF THE FAVORITE DRINKS
OF PRESIDENT JOHN F. KENNEDY.

INGREDIENTS

INSTRUCTIONS

2 OZ WHITE RUM

.75 OZ LIME JUICE

.75 OZ SIMPLE SYRUP

LIME (GARNISH)

GET SHAKER & ADD ICE ☐

ADD ALL INGREDIENTS ☐

SHAKE UNTIL CHILLED ☐

STRAIN INTO SERVING GLASS ☐

GARNISH W/ THIN LIME SLICE ☐

WHAT DO YOU THINK?

. . . .

. . . .

. . . .

. . . .

DRINK THIS AGAIN?   YES ☐   NO ☐   IF DESPERATE ☐

BONUS TRIVIA

THIS DRINK WAS SUPPOSEDLY INVENTED BY JENNINGS COX, AN AMERICAN MINING ENGINEER, WHILE IN CUBA IN 1898.

2 OZ
WHITE RUM

.75 OZ
LIME JUICE

.75 OZ
SIMPLE SYRUP

THIS ONE LOOKS GREAT IN A MARTINI GLASS.

YOU PRETTY MUCH HAVE EVERYTHING YOU NEED:

■ JUST MAKE SURE YOU HAVE A CUCUMBER

OH, AND YOU'LL ALSO NEED SOME CILANTRO (AND AN EGG)

THIS ONE IS ALLEGEDLY A FAVORITE OF JUSTIN TIMBERLAKE. NO JUDGMENT JUSTIN, BUT WEIRD PICK.

INGREDIENTS	INSTRUCTIONS
3 SLICES CUCUMBER	GET SHAKER ☐
6 CILANTRO LEAVES	ADD FIRST 3 INGREDIENTS ☐
.75 OZ SIMPLE SYRUP	MUDDLE UNTIL MIXED ☐
1.5 OZ BLANCO TEQUILA	FILL WITH ICE ☐
1 OZ LIME JUICE	ADD REMAINING INGREDIENTS ☐
.25 OZ EGG WHITE	SHAKE UNTIL CHILLED ☐
.75 OZ TRIPLE SEC	FILL SERVING GLASS W/ ICE ☐
CUCUMBER (GARNISH)	STRAIN INTO GLASS ☐
	GARNISH W/ CUCUMBER SLICE ☐

WHAT DO YOU THINK?

. . . .

DRINK THIS AGAIN?   YES ☐   NO ☐   IF DESPERATE ☐

IN 2002, A FEW MONTHS BEFORE THE RELEASE OF 'STAR WARS
EPISODE II: ATTACK OF THE CLONES,' LUCASFILM LEAKED THAT
THE MEMBERS OF *NSYNC WOULD BE MAKING CAMEOS (YAY?).
NATURALLY, THIS ANNOUNCEMENT WAS MET WITH IMMEDIATE
BACKLASH FROM FANS AND THE SCENES WERE ULTIMATELY CUT.

SO HEY, THE MOVIE COULD HAVE ACTUALLY BEEN WORSE.

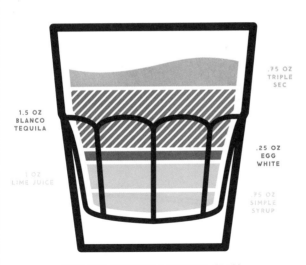

.75 OZ
TRIPLE
SEC

1.5 OZ
BLANCO
TEQUILA

.25 OZ
EGG
WHITE

1 OZ
LIME JUICE

.75 OZ
SIMPLE
SYRUP

THIS ONE DESERVES A LOWBALL GLASS.

YOU PRETTY MUCH HAVE EVERYTHING YOU NEED:

☐ JUST MAKE SURE YOU HAVE A SPARE EGG

AND MAYBE CHECK THE FRESHNESS OF THAT GINGER ALE

FIZZ DRINKS, POPULAR DURING THE EARLY 1900S, WERE ORIGINALLY SHAKEN FOR 15 MINUTES EACH.

INGREDIENTS	INSTRUCTIONS
2 OZ BLANCO TEQUILA	GET SHAKER & ADD ICE ☐
.75 OZ GRENADINE	ADD FIRST 4 INGREDIENTS ☐
1 SPLASH LEMON JUICE	SHAKE VIGOROUSLY ☐
1 EGG WHITE	FILL SERVING GLASS W/ ICE ☐
GINGER ALE	STRAIN INTO GLASS ☐
	TOP W/ GINGER ALE ☐
	STIR TO COMBINE ☐

WHAT DO YOU THINK?

. . . .

. . . .

DRINK THIS AGAIN?   YES ☐   NO ☐   IF DESPERATE ☐

BONUS TRIVIA

PHYSICISTS AT THE NATIONAL AUTONOMOUS UNIVERSITY OF
MEXICO HAVE MADE ARTIFICIAL DIAMONDS OUT OF TEQUILA.

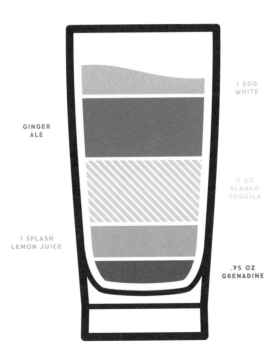

1 EGG
WHITE

GINGER
ALE

2 OZ
BLANCO
TEQUILA

1 SPLASH
LEMON JUICE

.75 OZ
GRENADINE

IF IT WERE US, WE'D USE A HIGHBALL GLASS.

YOU PRETTY MUCH HAVE EVERYTHING YOU NEED:

☐ JUST MAKE SURE YOU HAVE A LEMON

CHECK YOUR BAR FOR ANYTHING YOU'RE GETTING LOW ON, THOUGH

A CONFIRMED FAVORITE OF PATRICK CARNEY (OF THE BLACK KEYS). WE'VE HAD A FEW WITH HIM.

INGREDIENTS

2 OZ VODKA
4 OZ GRAPEFRUIT JUICE
LEMON (GARNISH)

INSTRUCTIONS

GET SERVING GLASS ☐
FILL WITH ICE ☐
ADD FIRST INGREDIENT ☐
TOP W/ GRAPEFRUIT JUICE ☐
STIR TO COMBINE ☐
GARNISH W/ LEMON TWIST ☐

WHAT DO YOU THINK?

. . . .

. . . .

. . . .

DRINK THIS AGAIN? YES ☐ NO ☐ IF DESPERATE ☐

BONUS TRIVIA

OVER 85% OF ALL GREYHOUNDS HAVE A SPECIAL UNIVERSAL
BLOOD TYPE THAT CAN BE USED IN ANY OTHER DOG, MAKING
THEM THE PERFECT BLOOD DONORS.

BONUS BONUS TRIVIA: THERE ARE TWELVE DIFFERENT
BLOOD TYPES IN DOGS, HENCE WHY THAT UNIVERSAL
BLOOD THING IS A BIG DEAL.

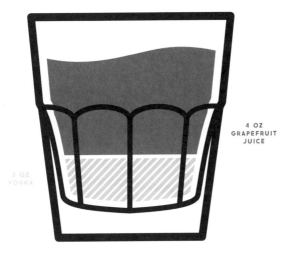

4 OZ
GRAPEFRUIT
JUICE

2 OZ
VODKA

WE'D RECOMMEND A LOWBALL GLASS FOR THIS ONE.

YOU PRETTY MUCH HAVE EVERYTHING YOU NEED:

☐ JUST MAKE SURE YOU HAVE A LIME

MAYBE CHECK ON THE FRESHNESS OF THAT LIME JUICE TOO

TWO STATES (UT & OK) STILL ALLOW EXECUTION BY
FIRING SQUAD UNDER CERTAIN CIRCUMSTANCES.

INGREDIENTS	INSTRUCTIONS
2 OZ BLANCO TEQUILA	GET SHAKER & ADD ICE ☐
.75 OZ LIME JUICE	ADD ALL INGREDIENTS ☐
.75 OZ GRENADINE	SHAKE UNTIL CHILLED ☐
5 DASH ANGOSTURA BITTERS	GET SERVING GLASS ☐
LIME (GARNISH)	FILL WITH ICE ☐
	STRAIN INTO GLASS ☐
	GARNISH W/ LIME SLICE ☐

WHAT DO YOU THINK?

. . . .

. . . .

. . . .

DRINK THIS AGAIN?   YES ☐   NO ☐   IF DESPERATE ☐

MAKE A FIRING SQUAD

THIS DRINK WAS FIRST DOCUMENTED IN 1932 BY CHARLES H. BAKER, A WORLD TRAVELER, HISTORIAN, & COCKTAIL WRITER.

HE DISCOVERED IT AT THE 'LA CUCARACHA' BAR IN MEXICO CITY. AND WHILE THE NAME OF THE BAR WAS ALREADY BAD ENOUGH, CHARLES DECIDED TO GIVE THIS DRINK A RATHER UNFORTUNATE NAME...SO WE FIXED IT A BIT.

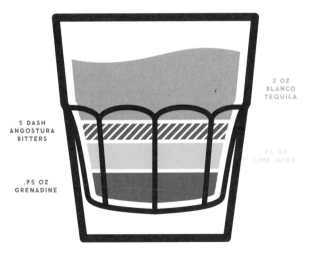

2 OZ
BLANCO
TEQUILA

5 DASH
ANGOSTURA
BITTERS

.75 OZ
LIME JUICE

.75 OZ
GRENADINE

A LOWBALL GLASS SUITS THIS ONE PERFECTLY.

FIRST THINGS FIRST, GO BUY SOME:

RYE WHISKEY

OH, AND MAYBE PICK UP A GRAPEFRUIT

THE TURN SIGNAL WAS PATENTED IN 1929, BUT IT DIDN'T
SEE WIDESPREAD USAGE UNTIL THE LATE 1940s.

INGREDIENTS

INSTRUCTIONS

2 OZ RYE WHISKEY — CHILL SERVING GLASS ☐

1 OZ GRAPEFRUIT JUICE — GET SHAKER & ADD ICE ☐

1 TBSP GRENADINE — ADD ALL INGREDIENTS ☐

GRAPEFRUIT (GARNISH) — SHAKE UNTIL CHILLED ☐

STRAIN INTO GLASS ☐

GARNISH W/ GRAPEFRUIT TWIST ☐

WHAT DO YOU THINK?

. . . .

. . . .

. . . .

DRINK THIS AGAIN?   YES ☐   NO ☐   IF DESPERATE ☐

BONUS TRIVIA

AFTER HIS TWO TERMS AS PRESIDENT, GEORGE WASHINGTON RETURNED TO MOUNT VERNON, WHERE HE OPENED HIS OWN DISTILLERY AND BEGAN MAKING RYE WHISKEY.

2 OZ
RYE
WHISKEY

1 TBSP
GRENADINE

1 OZ
GRAPEFRUIT
JUICE

USE A COUPE GLASS. TRUST US, IT'S WORTH IT.

YOU PRETTY MUCH HAVE EVERYTHING YOU NEED:

■ SO MAKE A DRINK ALREADY

CHECK YOUR BAR FOR ANYTHING YOU'RE GETTING LOW ON, THOUGH

WHAT MAKES IT REVERSE? WELL, BASICALLY, THE
PROPORTIONS OF THE INGREDIENTS ARE JUST FLIPPED.

INGREDIENTS	INSTRUCTIONS
2 OZ SWEET VERMOUTH	GET MIXING GLASS ☐
1 OZ RYE WHISKEY	FILL WITH ICE ☐
2 DASH ANGOSTURA BITTERS	ADD ALL INGREDIENTS ☐
2 DASH ORANGE BITTERS	STIR TO COMBINE ☐
	GET SERVING GLASS ☐
	FILL WITH ICE ☐
	STRAIN INTO GLASS ☐

WHAT DO YOU THINK?

. . . .

. . . .

. . . .

DRINK THIS AGAIN?   YES ☐   NO ☐   IF DESPERATE ☐

BONUS TRIVIA

THE LONGEST PALINDROME (A WORD THAT READS THE SAME BACKWARD AS IT DOES FORWARD) IN THE OXFORD ENGLISH DICTIONARY IS 'TATTARRATTAT,' COINED BY JAMES JOYCE IN THE 1922 NOVEL 'ULYSSES' FOR A KNOCK ON THE DOOR.

DAMMIT I'M MAD.

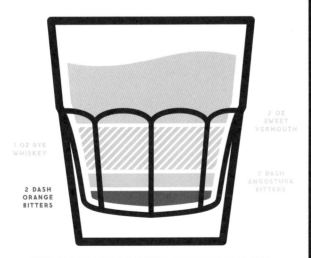

2 OZ SWEET VERMOUTH

1 OZ RYE WHISKEY

2 DASH ANGOSTURA BITTERS

2 DASH ORANGE BITTERS

WE'D RECOMMEND A LOWBALL GLASS FOR THIS ONE.

FIRST THINGS FIRST, GO BUY SOME:

RED WINE (PICK YOUR FAVORITE...OR A PRETTY LABEL)

PSST: YOU'LL ALSO NEED AN EGG FOR THIS ONE

HOW TO 'FLOAT' A LIQUID: CAREFULLY POUR IT OVER
THE BACK OF A SPOON SO IT CREATES A LAYER ON TOP.

INGREDIENTS	INSTRUCTIONS
2 OZ RYE WHISKEY	GET SHAKER & ADD ICE ☐
.75 OZ SIMPLE SYRUP	ADD FIRST 4 INGREDIENTS ☐
1 OZ LEMON JUICE	SHAKE UNTIL CHILLED ☐
1 EGG WHITE	FILL SERVING GLASS W/ ICE ☐
.5 OZ RED WINE	STRAIN INTO GLASS ☐
	FLOAT WINE ON TOP ☐

WHAT DO YOU THINK?

. . . .

. . . .

. . . .

. . . .

DRINK THIS AGAIN?　　YES ☐　　NO ☐　　IF DESPERATE ☐

IT'S BELIEVED THAT THIS COCKTAIL WAS ACTUALLY CREATED IN CHICAGO BY SIMON DIFFORD DURING THE LATE 1800s, AND ORIGINALLY KNOWN AS A CONTINENTAL SOUR.

LATER, AFTER THE DRINK GAINED POPULARITY IN THE NYC AREA, THE NAME MAGICALLY CHANGED.

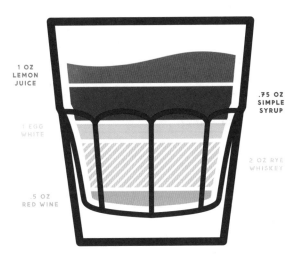

1 OZ
LEMON
JUICE

.75 OZ
SIMPLE
SYRUP

1 EGG
WHITE

2 OZ RYE
WHISKEY

.5 OZ
RED WINE

THIS ONE LOOKS GREAT IN A LOWBALL GLASS.

YOU PRETTY MUCH HAVE EVERYTHING YOU NEED:

■ JUST MAKE SURE YOU HAVE AN ORANGE

CHECK YOUR BAR FOR ANYTHING YOU'RE GETTING LOW ON, THOUGH

PRO-TIP: TRY KEEPING THAT BOTTLE OF VERMOUTH
IN THE FRIDGE. IT'LL STAY FRESH MUCH LONGER.

INGREDIENTS   **INSTRUCTIONS**

1.5 OZ RYE WHISKEY   CHILL SERVING GLASS ☐

1 OZ DRY VERMOUTH   GET SHAKER & ADD ICE ☐

.75 OZ LIME JUICE   ADD ALL INGREDIENTS ☐

.25 OZ GRENADINE   SHAKE UNTIL CHILLED ☐

1 DASH ORANGE BITTERS   STRAIN INTO GLASS ☐

ORANGE (GARNISH)   GARNISH W/ ORANGE TWIST ☐

WHAT DO YOU THINK?

· ·

· ·

· ·

· ·

DRINK THIS AGAIN?   YES ☐   NO ☐   IF DESPERATE ☐

BONUS TRIVIA

THIS DRINK WAS CREATED IN PARIS IN 1924 AS A HOMAGE TO THE AMERICANS STILL DRINKING DESPITE PROHIBITION. YOU KNOW, THE SCOFFLAWS.

1.5 OZ
RYE
WHISKEY

1 OZ
DRY
VERMOUTH

1 DASH
ORANGE
BITTERS

.25 OZ
GRENADINE

.75 OZ
LIME JUICE

A COUPE GLASS IS DEFINITELY YOUR BEST BET.

FIRST THINGS FIRST, GO BUY SOME:

■ COGNAC

OH, AND MAKE SURE YOU HAVE AN EXTRA LEMON

SARATOGA SPRINGS, NEW YORK, WAS ESSENTIALLY
THE 19TH CENTURY'S EQUIVALENT OF LAS VEGAS.

INGREDIENTS

■ 1 OZ COGNAC
■ 1 OZ TENNESSEE WHISKEY
■ 1 OZ SWEET VERMOUTH
■ 2 DASH ANGOSTURA BITTERS
■ LEMON (GARNISH)

INSTRUCTIONS

GET MIXING GLASS ☐
FILL WITH ICE ☐
ADD ALL INGREDIENTS ☐
STIR UNTIL CHILLED ☐
STRAIN INTO GLASS ☐
GARNISH W/ LEMON TWIST ☐

WHAT DO YOU THINK?

. . . .

. . . .

. . . .

DRINK THIS AGAIN?   YES ☐   NO ☐   IF DESPERATE ☐

BONUS TRIVIA

THERE ARE INSANELY STRICT LAWS ABOUT WHAT MAKES COGNAC, COGNAC. FOR EXAMPLE, IT HAS TO BE AGED IN BARRELS MADE OUT OF FRENCH OAK FROM ONE OF TWO SPECIFIC FORESTS.

1 OZ
COGNAC

1 OZ
SWEET
VERMOUTH

1 OZ
TENNESSEE
WHISKEY

2 DASH
ANGOSTURA
BITTERS

IF IT WERE US, WE'D GO WITH A COUPE GLASS.

YOU PRETTY MUCH HAVE EVERYTHING YOU NEED:

▮ JUST MAKE SURE YOU HAVE SOME CINNAMON

OH. AND YOU'LL ALSO NEED AN EGG

WHILE TYPICALLY USED SPARINGLY, ANGOSTURA BITTERS
ARE USED AS THE BASE IN THIS CREAMY DRINK.

INGREDIENTS	INSTRUCTIONS
1 OZ ANGOSTURA BITTERS	GET SHAKER ☐
1 OZ RYE WHISKEY	ADD ALL INGREDIENTS ☐
1 OZ CREAM	DRY SHAKE FOR 1 MIN ☐
.5 OZ SIMPLE SYRUP	ADD ICE & SHAKE AGAIN ☐
1 WHOLE EGG	STRAIN INTO SERVING GLASS ☐
CINNAMON (GARNISH)	GARNISH W/ CINNAMON ☐

WHAT DO YOU THINK?

. . . .

. . . .

. . . .

DRINK THIS AGAIN?　　YES ☐　　NO ☐　　IF DESPERATE ☐

BONUS TRIVIA

THE NAME FOR THE CITY OF PORTLAND, OREGON, WAS DECIDED WITH A COIN FLIP. IF IT HAD LANDED THE OTHER WAY, IT LIKELY WOULD HAVE BEEN CALLED LITTLE BOSTON.

1 WHOLE EGG

.5 OZ SIMPLE SYRUP

1 OZ ANGOSTURA BITTERS

1 OZ CREAM

1 OZ RYE WHISKEY

USE A COUPE GLASS. TRUST US, IT'S WORTH IT.

YOU PRETTY MUCH HAVE EVERYTHING YOU NEED:

- [ ] JUST MAKE SURE YOU HAVE SOME BRANDIED CHERRIES

CHECK YOUR BAR FOR ANYTHING YOU'RE GETTING LOW ON, THOUGH

FULL DISCLOSURE: THIS DRINK HAS SO MANY VARIATIONS
THAT WE JUST WENT WITH OUR FAVORITE.

INGREDIENTS

- 2 OZ RYE WHISKEY
- .75 OZ LEMON JUICE
- .75 OZ ORANGE JUICE
- 1 TSP GRENADINE
- BRANDIED CHERRY (GARNISH)

INSTRUCTIONS

- GET SHAKER & ADD ICE [ ]
- ADD ALL INGREDIENTS [ ]
- SHAKE UNTIL CHILLED [ ]
- STRAIN INTO GLASS [ ]
- GARNISH W/ CHERRY [ ]

WHAT DO YOU THINK?

. . . .

. . . .

. . . .

. . . .

DRINK THIS AGAIN?   YES [ ]   NO [ ]   IF DESPERATE [ ]

BONUS TRIVIA

THIS DRINK PROBABLY ORIGINATED IN BOSTON, BUT NO ONE REALLY KNOWS FOR SURE. GREAT STORY, HUH?

2 OZ RYE WHISKEY

.75 OZ LEMON JUICE

.75 OZ ORANGE JUICE

1 TSP GRENADINE

THIS ONE DEFINITELY CALLS FOR A MARTINI GLASS.

FIRST THINGS FIRST, GO BUY SOME:

CURAÇAO (FYI, IT'S PRONOUNCED CURE-AH-SOUW)

ALSO MAKE SURE YOU HAVE FINE SUGAR AND A LEMON

CREATED AROUND 1840 BY JOSEPH SANTINI — WHO APPARENTLY HAD WAY TOO MUCH TIME ON HIS HANDS.

INGREDIENTS	INSTRUCTIONS
2 OZ COGNAC	GET SERVING GLASS ☐
.5 TSP SIMPLE SYRUP	RIM W/ LEMON JUICE ☐
.25 TSP CURAÇAO	DIP IN SUGAR ☐
.25 TSP LEMON JUICE	PEEL HALF LEMON ☐
2 DASH ANGOSTURA BITTERS	LINE GLASS W/ PEEL ☐
SUGAR (FOR RIM)	GET MIXING GLASS ☐
LEMON (GARNISH)	ADD ICE & ALL LIQUIDS ☐
	STIR UNTIL CHILLED ☐
	STRAIN INTO SERVING GLASS ☐

WHAT DO YOU THINK?

. . . .

DRINK THIS AGAIN?   YES ☐   NO ☐   IF DESPERATE ☐

CRUSTAS ARE NAMED FOR THEIR (CRUSTY) SUGAR COATED RIMS.

2 OZ
COGNAC

.25 TSP
CURAÇAO

2 DASH
ANGOSTURA
BITTERS

.5 TSP
SIMPLE SYRUP

.25 TSP
LEMON JUICE

GO AHEAD AND GOOGLE WHAT A NICK & NORA GLASS IS.

YOU PRETTY MUCH HAVE EVERYTHING YOU NEED:

- [ ] JUST MAKE SURE YOU HAVE SOME EGGS

CHECK YOUR BAR FOR ANYTHING YOU'RE GETTING LOW ON, THOUGH

RATTLESNAKES BITE 7,000-8,000 PEOPLE EACH YEAR,
BUT (THANKS TO ANTIVENOMS) ONLY 5-6 PROVE FATAL.

INGREDIENTS	INSTRUCTIONS
2 OZ RYE WHISKEY	GET SHAKER [ ]
.75 OZ LEMON JUICE	ADD ALL INGREDIENTS [ ]
.75 OZ EGG WHITES	DRY SHAKE FOR 1 MINUTE [ ]
.5 OZ SIMPLE SYRUP	ADD ICE & SHAKE AGAIN [ ]
.25 OZ ABSINTHE	STRAIN INTO SERVING GLASS [ ]

WHAT DO YOU THINK?

. . . .

. . . .

. . . .

DRINK THIS AGAIN?   YES [ ]   NO [ ]   IF DESPERATE [ ]

BONUS TRIVIA

THE SAVOY COCKTAIL BOOK PROBABLY SAYS IT BEST: 'THIS DRINK WILL EITHER KILL A RATTLESNAKE, CURE THEIR BITE, OR MAKE YOU SEE THEM.'

2 OZ
RYE
WHISKEY

.25 OZ
ABSINTHE

.5 OZ
SIMPLE SYRUP

.75 OZ
LEMON
JUICE

.75 OZ
EGG WHITES

IT'S WAY BETTER IN A COUPE GLASS.

FIRST THINGS FIRST, GO BUY SOME:

CAMPARI

OH, AND YOU'LL ALSO NEED AN ORANGE

RUMORED TO BE ANDY GARCIA'S FAVORITE DRINK. YOU KNOW, IN ALL OF THOSE ANDY GARCIA GOSSIP CIRCLES.

INGREDIENTS

INSTRUCTIONS

1 OZ DRY GIN

1 OZ CAMPARI

1 OZ SWEET VERMOUTH

ORANGE (GARNISH)

GET SHAKER & ADD ICE ☐

ADD ALL INGREDIENTS ☐

SHAKE UNTIL CHILLED ☐

FILL SERVING GLASS W/ ICE ☐

STRAIN INTO GLASS ☐

GARNISH W/ ORANGE TWIST ☐

WHAT DO YOU THINK?

. . . .

. . . .

. . . .

DRINK THIS AGAIN? YES ☐ NO ☐ IF DESPERATE ☐

BONUS TRIVIA

THIS COCKTAIL WAS LIKELY CREATED IN FLORENCE, ITALY, AT A PLACE CALLED 'CAFÉ CASONI.' SORRY, IT'S SINCE CLOSED. BUT NEVER FEAR, THERE'S A PLAQUE.

SO THE NEXT TIME YOU'RE STOPPING THROUGH FLORENCE, STOP BY 'GIACOSA CAFE' (THAT'S WHAT IT'S CALLED NOW) AND LOOK AT IT, I GUESS.

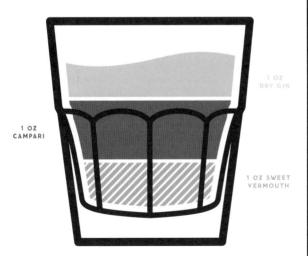

1 OZ
DRY GIN

1 OZ
CAMPARI

1 OZ SWEET
VERMOUTH

WE'D RECOMMEND A LOWBALL GLASS FOR THIS ONE.

YOU PRETTY MUCH HAVE EVERYTHING YOU NEED:

■ JUST MAKE SURE YOU HAVE AN ORANGE HANDY

■ AND MAYBE CHECK THE FRESHNESS OF THAT ORANGE JUICE

STRAWBERRIES AREN'T TECHNICALLY BERRIES,
AND YET ORANGES SECRETLY ARE.

INGREDIENTS	INSTRUCTIONS
1 OZ CAMPARI	GET SERVING GLASS ☐
3 OZ ORANGE JUICE	FILL WITH ICE ☐
ORANGE (GARNISH)	POUR IN CAMPARI ☐
	TOP W/ ORANGE JUICE ☐
	STIR TO COMBINE ☐
	GARNISH W/ ORANGE SLICE ☐

WHAT DO YOU THINK?

. . . .

. . . .

. . . .

. . . .

DRINK THIS AGAIN?   YES ☐   NO ☐   IF DESPERATE ☐

NAMED AFTER GIUSEPPE GARIBALDI, THE ITALIAN GENERAL WHO
HELPED UNIFY ITALY IN 1871. CAMPARI = NORTH. OJ = SOUTH.

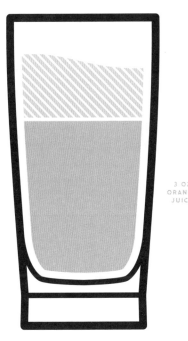

1 OZ
CAMPARI

3 OZ
ORANGE
JUICE

YOU SHOULD PROBABLY USE A HIGHBALL GLASS.

# MAKE A NEGRONI SBAGLIATO

FIRST THINGS FIRST, GO BUY SOME:

☐ PROSECCO (YES, IT'S DIFFERENT THAN CHAMPAGNE)

OH, AND MAKE SURE YOU HAVE AN EXTRA ORANGE TOO

A CLASSIC ITALIAN APERITIVO (AKA: A PRE-MEAL DRINK
SPECIFICALLY MEANT TO WHET YOUR APPETITE).

INGREDIENTS

☐ 1 OZ CAMPARI
☐ 1 OZ SWEET VERMOUTH
☐ PROSECCO
☐ ORANGE (GARNISH)

INSTRUCTIONS

GET SERVING GLASS ☐
FILL WITH ICE ☐
ADD FIRST 2 INGREDIENTS ☐
TOP WITH PROSECCO ☐
STIR TO COMBINE ☐
GARNISH W/ ORANGE TWIST ☐

WHAT DO YOU THINK?

. . . .

. . . .

. . . .

DRINK THIS AGAIN?   YES ☐   NO ☐   IF DESPERATE ☐

BONUS TRIVIA

THIS DRINK, AS LEGEND WOULD HAVE IT, WAS ACCIDENTALLY CREATED WHEN A BARTENDER USED SPARKLING WINE INSTEAD OF GIN WHEN MAKING A NEGRONI.

IN FACT, THE ITALIAN WORD 'SBAGLIATO' MORE OR LESS TRANSLATES TO 'MISTAKE' IN ENGLISH, A NOD TO THE DRINK'S (ACCIDENTAL) ORIGIN.

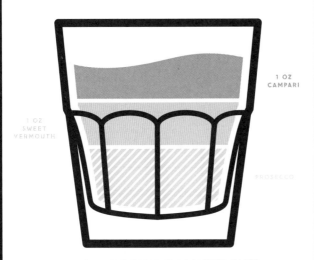

1 OZ
CAMPARI

1 OZ
SWEET
VERMOUTH

PROSECCO

CAMPARI LOOKS GREAT IN A LOWBALL GLASS.

YOU PRETTY MUCH HAVE EVERYTHING YOU NEED:

■ JUST MAKE SURE YOU HAVE SOME STRAWBERRIES

CHECK YOUR BAR FOR ANYTHING YOU'RE GETTING LOW ON, THOUGH

ONCE A SCENT IS IDENTIFIED, A BLOODHOUND CAN
FOLLOW IT FOR MORE THAN 130 MILES.

INGREDIENTS	INSTRUCTIONS
■ 3 STRAWBERRIES	CHILL SERVING GLASS ☐
■ .75 OZ DRY VERMOUTH	GET SHAKER ☐
■ .75 OZ SWEET VERMOUTH	MUDDLE STRAWBERRIES ☐
■ 1.5 OZ DRY GIN	FILL WITH ICE ☐
■ STRAWBERRY (GARNISH)	ADD OTHER INGREDIENTS ☐
	SHAKE UNTIL CHILLED ☐
	STRAIN INTO SERVING GLASS ☐
	GARNISH W/ STRAWBERRY ☐

WHAT DO YOU THINK?

. . . .

. . . .

DRINK THIS AGAIN?   YES ☐   NO ☐   IF DESPERATE ☐

BONUS TRIVIA

ON JANUARY 16TH, 2016, A BLOODHOUND NAMED LUDIVINE ACCIDENTALLY JOINED A HALF MARATHON AFTER HER OWNER LET HER OUTSIDE. SHE RAN ALL 13.1 MILES AND FINISHED 7TH.

1.5 OZ
DRY GIN

.75 OZ
DRY
VERMOUTH

.75 OZ
SWEET VERMOUTH

IF IT WERE US, WE'D GO WITH A COUPE GLASS.

FIRST THINGS FIRST, GO BUY SOME:

ANISETTE LIQUEUR

OH, AND MAKE SURE YOU HAVE ORANGES WHILE YOU'RE AT IT

THIS IS SUPPOSEDLY A FAVORITE DRINK OF BENEDICT
CUMBERBATCH. IF YOU SEE HIM, VERIFY THAT FOR US.

INGREDIENTS	INSTRUCTIONS
3 OZ PROSECCO	GET SERVING GLASS ☐
2 OZ ANISETTE LIQUEUR	FILL WITH ICE ☐
CLUB SODA	ADD FIRST 2 INGREDIENTS ☐
ORANGE (GARNISH)	TOP W/ CLUB SODA ☐
	STIR TO COMBINE ☐
	GARNISH W/ ORANGE SLICE ☐

WHAT DO YOU THINK?

. . . .

. . . .

. . . .

. . . .

DRINK THIS AGAIN?   YES ☐   NO ☐   IF DESPERATE ☐

BONUS TRIVIA

IN VENICE, THE WORD 'SPRITZ' IS PRONOUNCED 'SPRISS'.

2 OZ
ANISETTE
LIQUEUR

CLUB
SODA

3 OZ
PROSECCO

USE A WINE GLASS, YOU'LL FEEL EXTRA FANCY.

YOU PRETTY MUCH HAVE EVERYTHING YOU NEED:

■ JUST MAKE SURE YOU HAVE SOME MINT

OH, AND YOU'LL NEED A LEMON TOO

A RAISIN IN CHAMPAGNE WILL GO FROM THE TOP OF
THE GLASS TO THE BOTTOM AND BACK. OVER & OVER.

INGREDIENTS

■ .5 OZ SIMPLE SYRUP
■ 6 MINT LEAVES
■ 1 DASH ANGOSTURA BITTERS
■ .5 OZ COGNAC
■ CHAMPAGNE
■ LEMON (GARNISH)

INSTRUCTIONS

GET SHAKER ☐
ADD FIRST 3 INGREDIENTS ☐
MUDDLE LIGHTLY ☐
FILL WITH ICE ☐
POUR IN COGNAC & SHAKE ☐
FILL SERVING GLASS W/ ICE ☐
STRAIN INTO GLASS ☐
TOP WITH CHAMPAGNE ☐
GARNISH W/ LEMON TWIST ☐

WHAT DO YOU THINK?

. . . .

DRINK THIS AGAIN?　　YES ☐　NO ☐　IF DESPERATE ☐

BONUS TRIVIA

THE AMOUNT OF PRESSURE INSIDE A CHAMPAGNE BOTTLE IS OVER 90 POUNDS PER SQUARE INCH. THAT'S THREE TIMES THE AMOUNT INSIDE OF A CAR TIRE.

DUE TO ALL OF THIS PRESSURE, YOU'RE MORE LIKELY TO BE KILLED IN A CHAMPAGNE-RELATED ACCIDENT THAN YOU ARE FROM A POISONOUS SPIDER BITE.

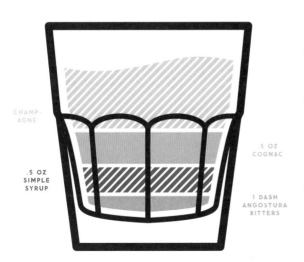

CHAMP-
AGNE

.5 OZ
COGNAC

.5 OZ
SIMPLE
SYRUP

1 DASH
ANGOSTURA
BITTERS

THIS ONE IS SURPRISINGLY SUITED FOR A LOWBALL.

FIRST THINGS FIRST, GO BUY SOME:

█ COFFEE LIQUEUR

AND MAYBE CHECK THE FRESHNESS OF THAT CREAM

SAVED FROM RELATIVE OBSCURITY BY THE RELEASE
OF THE 1998 FILM 'THE BIG LEBOWSKI.'

INGREDIENTS

INSTRUCTIONS

INGREDIENTS	INSTRUCTIONS	
█ 1 OZ VODKA	GET SERVING GLASS	☐
█ 1 OZ COFFEE LIQUEUR	FILL WITH ICE	☐
█ 1 OZ CREAM	ADD FIRST 2 INGREDIENTS	☐
	STIR TO COMBINE	☐
	GENTLY TOP W/ CREAM	☐

WHAT DO YOU THINK?

. . . .

. . . .

. . . .

. . . .

DRINK THIS AGAIN?   YES ☐   NO ☐   IF DESPERATE ☐

BONUS TRIVIA

THIS COCKTAIL WAS FIRST CREATED IN 1949 BY GUSTAVE TOPS, AT THE 'HOTEL METROPOLE' IN BRUSSELS. IT WAS ORIGINALLY MADE IN HONOR OF PERLE MESTA, THE U.S. AMBASSADOR TO LUXEMBOURG AT THE TIME.

ABSOLUTELY NONE OF THESE THINGS HAVE ANYTHING TO DO WITH RUSSIA, EXCEPT FOR (STEREOTYPICALLY) THE VODKA.

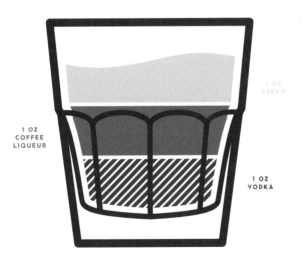

1 OZ CREAM

1 OZ COFFEE LIQUEUR

1 OZ VODKA

YOU SHOULD OBVIOUSLY USE A LOWBALL GLASS.

YOU PRETTY MUCH HAVE EVERYTHING YOU NEED:

JUST MAKE SURE YOUR ORANGE JUICE IS STILL GOOD

CHECK YOUR BAR FOR ANYTHING YOU'RE GETTING LOW ON, THOUGH

IT TURNS OUT THAT THE BRONX COCKTAIL IS NAMED
AFTER THE ZOO, AND NOT THE BOROUGH.

INGREDIENTS

INGREDIENTS	INSTRUCTIONS
2 OZ DRY GIN	CHILL SERVING GLASS ☐
.25 OZ DRY VERMOUTH	GET SHAKER & ADD ICE ☐
.25 OZ SWEET VERMOUTH	ADD ALL INGREDIENTS ☐
1 OZ ORANGE JUICE	SHAKE UNTIL CHILLED ☐
1 DASH ORANGE BITTERS	STRAIN INTO GLASS ☐

WHAT DO YOU THINK?

. . . .

. . . .

. . . .

DRINK THIS AGAIN?   YES ☐   NO ☐   IF DESPERATE ☐

BONUS TRIVIA

IN 1934, THIS DRINK WAS RANKED THIRD IN 'THE WORLD'S TEN MOST FAMOUS COCKTAILS' LIST BEHIND THE MARTINI AND THE MANHATTAN. OH, HOW THINGS HAVE CHANGED.

2 OZ
DRY GIN

1 OZ
ORANGE
JUICE

1 DASH
ORANGE
BITTERS

.25 OZ
DRY
VERMOUTH

.25 OZ
SWEET
VERMOUTH

THIS ONE LOOKS GREAT IN A COUPE GLASS.

FIRST THINGS FIRST, GO BUY SOME:

■ PINEAPPLE JUICE (PRO-TIP: GET THE REAL STUFF)

UNLESS YOU WANT YOUR DRINK TO TASTE LIKE SUNSCREEN

NAMED AFTER THE SILENT ERA'S BEST-KNOWN AND
MOST-BELOVED ACTRESS.

INGREDIENTS

INSTRUCTIONS

■ 2 OZ WHITE RUM

■ 2 OZ PINEAPPLE JUICE

■ .25 OZ GRENADINE

■ .25 OZ MARASCHINO LIQUEUR

GET SHAKER & ADD ICE ☐

ADD ALL INGREDIENTS ☐

SHAKE UNTIL CHILLED ☐

STRAIN INTO GLASS ☐

WHAT DO YOU THINK?

. . . .

. . . .

. . . .

. . . .

. . . .

DRINK THIS AGAIN?   YES ☐   NO ☐   IF DESPERATE ☐

WHILE SHE WAS KNOWN AS 'AMERICA'S SWEETHEART,'
MARY PICKFORD WAS ACTUALLY BORN IN CANADA.

2 OZ
WHITE
RUM

.25 OZ
GRENADINE

.25 OZ
MARASCHINO
LIQUEUR

2 OZ
PINEAPPLE
JUICE

USE A COUPE GLASS. TRUST US, IT'S WORTH IT.

FIRST THINGS FIRST, GO BUY SOME:

☐ MELON LIQUEUR

DON'T FORGET TO ADD THIS TO YOUR INVENTORY LIST

GOOSE, TOOTH, AND FOOT ARE THE ONLY ENGLISH
WORDS WHERE 'OO' CHANGES TO 'EE' FOR THE PLURAL.

INGREDIENTS	INSTRUCTIONS
1 OZ VODKA	GET SERVING GLASS ☐
1 OZ MELON LIQUEUR	FILL WITH ICE ☐
2 OZ PINEAPPLE JUICE	ADD ALL INGREDIENTS ☐
	STIR TO COMBINE ☐

WHAT DO YOU THINK?

. . . .

. . . .

. . . .

. . . .

. . . .

DRINK THIS AGAIN?   YES ☐   NO ☐   IF DESPERATE ☐

BONUS TRIVIA

MOST BABY GEESE ARE INCREDIBLY IMPRESSIONABLE AND WILL FOLLOW VIRTUALLY ANYTHING THAT MOVES, THINKING IT TO BE THEIR MOTHER. THEY HAVE BEEN KNOWN TO FOLLOW DOGS, DUCKS, AND HUMANS (AMONG OTHER THINGS).

THINK ABOUT THIS WHILE YOU DRINK, I GUESS.

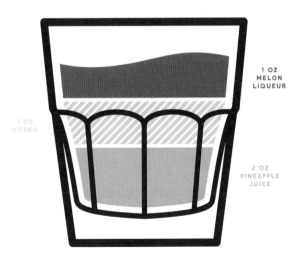

1 OZ
MELON
LIQUEUR

1 OZ
VODKA

2 OZ
PINEAPPLE
JUICE

WE'D RECOMMEND A LOWBALL GLASS FOR THIS ONE.

YOU PRETTY MUCH HAVE EVERYTHING YOU NEED:

JUST MAKE SURE YOU HAVE A LEMON

OH, AND YOU'LL ALSO NEED A BRANDIED CHERRY

THE NEVADA STATE PRISON HAD A CASINO FOR THE INMATES UNTIL 1967 WHEN A NEW WARDEN CLOSED IT.

INGREDIENTS	INSTRUCTIONS
1.5 OZ OLD TOM GIN	CHILL SERVING GLASS ☐
.25 OZ MARASCHINO LIQUEUR	GET SHAKER ☐
.25 OZ ORANGE BITTERS	ADD ALL INGREDIENTS ☐
.25 OZ LEMON JUICE	FILL WITH ICE ☐
LEMON (GARNISH)	SHAKE UNTIL CHILLED ☐
BRANDIED CHERRY (GARNISH)	STRAIN INTO GLASS ☐
	GARNISH W/ CHERRY ☐
	ADD LEMON TWIST ☐

WHAT DO YOU THINK?

. . . .

. . . .

DRINK THIS AGAIN?   YES ☐   NO ☐   IF DESPERATE ☐

BONUS TRIVIA

THE F-WORD IS SAID 435 TIMES DURING THE 1995 FILM 'CASINO'.
THAT'S AN AVERAGE OF 2.4 TIMES A MINUTE.

1.5 OZ
OLD TOM GIN

.25 OZ
MARASCHINO
LIQUEUR

.25 OZ
ORANGE
BITTERS

.25 OZ
LEMON JUICE

THIS ONE DEFINITELY CALLS FOR A MARTINI GLASS.

FIRST THINGS FIRST, GO BUY SOME:

■ COCA-COLA

CHECK YOUR BAR FOR ANYTHING YOU'RE GETTING LOW ON, THOUGH

> RUMORED TO BE A FAVORITE OF TAYLOR SWIFT
> (WE HEAR SHE USES DIET COKE, THOUGH).

INGREDIENTS   INSTRUCTIONS

■ 1.5 OZ DARK RUM   GET SERVING GLASS ☐
■ 3 OZ COCA-COLA   FILL WITH ICE ☐
                              ADD ALL INGREDIENTS ☐
                                  STIR TO COMBINE ☐

WHAT DO YOU THINK?

. . . .

. . . .

. . . .

. . . .

. . . .

DRINK THIS AGAIN?   YES ☐   NO ☐   IF DESPERATE ☐

THIS DRINK IS SAID TO HAVE BEEN CREATED IN 1900, DURING
THE END OF THE AMERICAN OCCUPATION OF CUBA. IT COMBINED
THE SPECIALTIES OF THE UNITED STATES (COCA-COLA) AND
CUBA (CUBAN RUM) TO SYMBOLIZE THE UNION BETWEEN THE
TWO NATIONS.

THE NAME EVEN TRANSLATES TO 'FREE CUBA.'

3 OZ
COCA-COLA

1.5 OZ
DARK RUM

WE'D RECOMMEND A LOWBALL GLASS FOR THIS ONE.

MAKE A FLORAL

MAKE A FLORAL

YOU PRETTY MUCH HAVE EVERYTHING YOU NEED:

■ JUST MAKE SURE YOU HAVE A CUCUMBER

OH, AND YOU'LL ALSO NEED SOME ROSEMARY (AND THYME)

THE NAME FOR ROSEMARY IS DERIVED FROM THE
LATIN 'ROS MARINUS,' MEANING 'DEW OF THE SEA.'

INGREDIENTS   INSTRUCTIONS

■ .75 OZ LIME JUICE   GET SHAKER ☐
■ .75 OZ SIMPLE SYRUP   ADD FIRST 5 INGREDIENTS ☐
■ 1 CUCUMBER SLICE   MUDDLE UNTIL MIXED ☐
■ 1 ROSEMARY SPRIG   FILL WITH ICE ☐
■ 1 THYME SPRIG   ADD VODKA ☐
■ 1.5 OZ VODKA   SHAKE UNTIL CHILLED ☐
■ THYME SPRIG (GARNISH)   STRAIN INTO GLASS ☐
■ CUCUMBER (GARNISH)   GARNISH W/ THYME ☐
                                    ADD CUCUMBER SLICE ☐

WHAT DO YOU THINK?

. . . .

DRINK THIS AGAIN?   YES ☐   NO ☐   IF DESPERATE ☐

BONUS TRIVIA

IF YOU'RE EVER OUT OF ONIONS, IT'S SAID THAT YOU CAN
USE TULIP BULBS AS A SUBSTITUTE IN A RECIPE.

WHO WANTS SOME TULIP RINGS?

1.5 OZ
VODKA

.75 OZ
SIMPLE
SYRUP

.75 OZ
LIME JUICE

USE A COUPE GLASS. TRUST US, IT'S WORTH IT.

YOU PRETTY MUCH HAVE EVERYTHING YOU NEED:

▮ JUST MAKE SURE YOU HAVE AN EXTRA LEMON

CHECK YOUR BAR FOR ANYTHING YOU'RE GETTING LOW ON, THOUGH

THE FIRST PRINTED RECIPE FOR ONE APPEARED IN 'BETTY CROCKER'S NEW PICTURE COOKBOOK' IN 1961.

INGREDIENTS

▮ .75 OZ VODKA
▮ .75 OZ DRY GIN
▮ .75 OZ WHITE RUM
▮ .75 OZ BLANCO TEQUILA
▮ 1.5 OZ TRIPLE SEC
▮ .75 OZ LEMON JUICE
▮ 2 OZ COCA-COLA
▮ LEMON (GARNISH)

INSTRUCTIONS

GET SERVING GLASS ☐
FILL WITH ICE ☐
ADD ALL INGREDIENTS ☐
STIR TO COMBINE ☐
GARNISH W/ LEMON WEDGE ☐

WHAT DO YOU THINK?

. . . .

. . . .

DRINK THIS AGAIN?   YES ☐   NO ☐   IF DESPERATE ☐

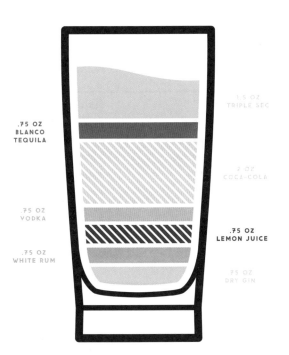

BONUS TRIVIA

LONG ISLAND CONTAINS THE PRICIEST ZIP CODE IN AMERICA. THE
MEDIAN HOME PRICE IN 11962 (SAGAPONACK, NY) IS $8.5M.

1.5 OZ
TRIPLE SEC

.75 OZ
BLANCO
TEQUILA

2 OZ
COCA-COLA

.75 OZ
VODKA

.75 OZ
LEMON JUICE

.75 OZ
WHITE RUM

.75 OZ
DRY GIN

YOU SHOULD PROBABLY USE A HIGHBALL GLASS.

MAKE A SIDECAR

YOU PRETTY MUCH HAVE EVERYTHING YOU NEED:

JUST MAKE SURE YOU HAVE SOME SUGAR

OH, AND YOU'LL ALSO NEED AN ORANGE

A FAVORITE DRINK OF RACHEL MADDOW. YOU CAN EVEN
WATCH HER MAKE ONE ON YOUTUBE FOR SOME REASON.

INGREDIENTS

- 1.5 OZ COGNAC
- .75 OZ TRIPLE SEC
- .75 OZ LEMON JUICE
- SUGAR (GLASS RIM)
- ORANGE (GARNISH)

INSTRUCTIONS

- GET SERVING GLASS ☐
- RIM W/ LEMON JUICE ☐
- DIP IN SUGAR ☐
- GET SHAKER & ADD ICE ☐
- ADD ALL INGREDIENTS ☐
- SHAKE UNTIL CHILLED ☐
- STRAIN INTO GLASS ☐
- GARNISH W/ ORANGE TWIST ☐

WHAT DO YOU THINK?

. . . .

. . . .

DRINK THIS AGAIN?   YES ☐   NO ☐   IF DESPERATE ☐

IN BARTENDING SLANG, A 'SIDECAR' REFERS TO ANY LIQUID
LEFT IN A SHAKER AFTER THE MAIN DRINK IS POURED.

1.5 OZ
COGNAC

.75 OZ
TRIPLE SEC

.75 OZ
LEMON JUICE

THIS ONE LOOKS GREAT IN A MARTINI GLASS.

MAKE A COLONY COCKTAIL

YOU PRETTY MUCH HAVE EVERYTHING YOU NEED:

SO USE THIS TIME TO THANK US (@BRASSMONKEYGOODS)

JUST MAKE SURE THAT YOU HAVE A GRAPEFRUIT FIRST

CREATED AT 'COLONY,' A PROHIBITION-ERA SPEAKEASY
IN NEW YORK CITY, BY MARCO HATTEM.

INGREDIENTS

- 1.5 OZ DRY GIN
- .25 OZ MARASCHINO LIQUEUR
- 1 OZ GRAPEFRUIT JUICE
- GRAPEFRUIT (GARNISH)

INSTRUCTIONS

- CHILL SERVING GLASS ☐
- GET SHAKER ☐
- FILL WITH ICE ☐
- ADD ALL INGREDIENTS ☐
- SHAKE UNTIL CHILLED ☐
- STRAIN INTO SERVING GLASS ☐
- GARNISH W/ GRAPEFRUIT TWIST ☐

WHAT DO YOU THINK?

. . . .

. . . .

DRINK THIS AGAIN?   YES ☐   NO ☐   IF DESPERATE ☐

BONUS TRIVIA

AT 'COLONY,' THEY KEPT ALL OF THEIR LIQUOR IN THE ELEVATOR. SO IF FEDERAL AGENTS EVER RAIDED THE PLACE, THEY SIMPLY SENT IT TO THE BASEMENT.

1.5 OZ
DRY GIN

.25 OZ
MARASCHINO
LIQUEUR

1 OZ
GRAPEFRUIT
JUICE

IF IT WERE US, WE'D GO WITH A COUPE GLASS.

FIRST THINGS FIRST, GO BUY SOME:

GINGER BEER

CHECK YOUR BAR FOR ANYTHING YOU'RE GETTING LOW ON, THOUGH

THE LONG HAIR ON THE LOWER LEGS OF SOME HORSES
(LIKE CLYDESDALES) ARE KNOWN AS FEATHERS.

INGREDIENTS   **INSTRUCTIONS**

4 OZ GINGER BEER   GET SERVING GLASS ☐
1.5 OZ TENNESSEE WHISKEY   FILL WITH ICE ☐
4 DASH ANGOSTURA BITTERS   ADD INGREDIENTS ☐
1 SPLASH LEMON JUICE   STIR TO COMBINE ☐

WHAT DO YOU THINK?

. . . .

. . . .

. . . .

. . . .

DRINK THIS AGAIN?   YES ☐   NO ☐   IF DESPERATE ☐

BONUS TRIVIA

CREATED IN LAWRENCE, KS, IN THE 1990s. SADLY IT'S ONLY POPULAR IN THE KANSAS CITY AREA. LET'S CHANGE THAT.

4 OZ
GINGER
BEER

1.5 OZ
TENNESSEE
WHISKEY

4 DASH
ANGOSTURA
BITTERS

1 SPLASH
LEMON
JUICE

YOU SHOULD PROBABLY USE A HIGHBALL GLASS.

YOU PRETTY MUCH HAVE EVERYTHING YOU NEED:

JUST CHECK THE FRESHNESS OF THAT ORANGE JUICE

AND FOR BEST RESULTS, MAKE SURE IT'S PULP FREE

IT'S THE FIRST DRINK IN THE 1930 'SAVOY COCKTAIL BOOK.' DON'T GET TOO EXCITED. IT WAS ALPHABETICAL.

INGREDIENTS	INSTRUCTIONS
.5 OZ DRY GIN	GET SHAKER & ADD ICE ☐
.25 OZ LILLET BLANC	ADD ALL INGREDIENTS ☐
.25 ORANGE JUICE	SHAKE UNTIL CHILLED ☐
1 DASH ANGOSTURA BITTERS	STRAIN INTO GLASS ☐

WHAT DO YOU THINK?

. . . .

. . . .

. . . .

. . . .

. . . .

DRINK THIS AGAIN?   YES ☐   NO ☐   IF DESPERATE ☐

BONUS TRIVIA

ASKED TO DESCRIBE 'DOWNTON ABBEY,' STAR HUGH BONNEVILLE
SAID 'IT'S 'BREAKING BAD' WITH TEA INSTEAD OF METH.'

.5 OZ
DRY GIN

1 DASH
ANGOSTURA
BITTERS

.25 OZ
ORANGE JUICE

.25 OZ
LILLET BLANC

USE A MARTINI GLASS, YOU WON'T REGRET IT.

YOU PRETTY MUCH HAVE EVERYTHING YOU NEED:

■ JUST MAKE SURE YOU HAVE (NON-EXPIRED) CREAM

CHECK YOUR BAR FOR ANYTHING YOU'RE GETTING LOW ON, THOUGH

CREATED AT 'THE BLUE BLAZER' IN 1952. THEY WERE
KNOWN FOR SETTING WHISKEY ON FIRE. GET IT? BLAZER.

INGREDIENTS   **INSTRUCTIONS**

■ 2 OZ COFFEE LIQUEUR   GET SERVING GLASS ☐

■ 2 OZ CREAM   FILL WITH ICE ☐

■ CLUB SODA   ADD FIRST 2 INGREDIENTS ☐

                                   TOP W/ CLUB SODA ☐

                                   STIR TO COMBINE ☐

WHAT DO YOU THINK?

. . . .

. . . .

. . . .

. . . .

DRINK THIS AGAIN?   YES ☐   NO ☐   IF DESPERATE ☐

BONUS TRIVIA

IT'S NAMED AFTER TWO REGULARS AT THE BAR, SMITH AND CURRAN. IT WAS JUST LOUD, SO HIS NAME WAS MISHEARD.

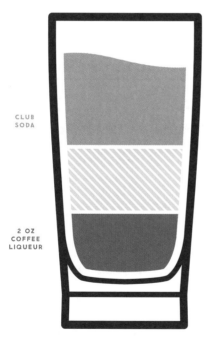

CLUB
SODA

2 OZ
CREAM

2 OZ
COFFEE
LIQUEUR

YOU SHOULD PROBABLY USE A HIGHBALL GLASS.

YOU PRETTY MUCH HAVE EVERYTHING YOU NEED:

JUST CHECK YOUR FRIDGE FOR AN EGG

OH, AND MAKE SURE YOU HAVE A LEMON WHILE YOU'RE AT IT

SURPRISINGLY, IT'S NOT NAMED AFTER THAT WOMAN
THAT'S ALWAYS ASKING TO SPEAK TO YOUR MANAGER.

INGREDIENTS   **INSTRUCTIONS**

2 OZ DRY GIN   GET SHAKER ☐

.5 OZ TRIPLE SEC   ADD ALL INGREDIENTS ☐

.5 OZ LEMON JUICE   DRY SHAKE FOR 1 MINUTE ☐

1 EGG WHITE   ADD ICE & SHAKE AGAIN ☐

LEMON (GARNISH)   STRAIN INTO SERVING GLASS ☐

                            GARNISH W/ LEMON TWIST ☐

WHAT DO YOU THINK?

. . . .

. . . .

. . . .

DRINK THIS AGAIN?   YES ☐   NO ☐   IF DESPERATE ☐

2 OZ
DRY GIN

.5 OZ
LEMON
JUICE

.5 OZ
TRIPLE
SEC

1 EGG
WHITE

USE A COUPE GLASS. TRUST US, IT'S WORTH IT.

YOU PRETTY MUCH HAVE EVERYTHING YOU NEED:

▪ JUST MAKE SURE YOU HAVE A LIME

CHECK YOUR BAR FOR ANYTHING YOU'RE GETTING LOW ON, THOUGH

CREATED BY WES PRICE IN 1941. HE ONLY COMBINED THE
TWO INGREDIENTS BECAUSE NEITHER WERE SELLING.

INGREDIENTS	INSTRUCTIONS
2 OZ VODKA	GET SERVING GLASS & ADD ICE ☐
.5 OZ LIME JUICE	ADD FIRST 2 INGREDIENTS ☐
5 OZ GINGER BEER	TOP WITH GINGER BEER ☐
LIME (GARNISH)	STIR TO COMBINE ☐
	GARNISH W/ LIME SLICE ☐

WHAT DO YOU THINK?

. . . .

. . . .

. . . .

. . . .

DRINK THIS AGAIN?   YES ☐   NO ☐   IF DESPERATE ☐

BONUS TRIVIA

AT THE HEIGHT OF MCCARTHYISM IN HOLLYWOOD, WHEN
ANYONE WITH RUSSIAN TIES WAS BLACKLISTED, A RUMOR
BEGAN CIRCULATING THAT SMIRNOFF VODKA WAS INVOLVED
IN A HUGE ANTI-AMERICAN CONSPIRACY. BARTENDERS EVEN
BEGAN TO BOYCOTT MAKING THE MOSCOW MULE.

LUCKILY THE CLAIMS WERE FALSE (OF COURSE).

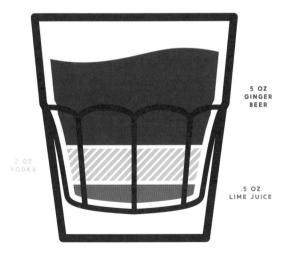

5 OZ
GINGER
BEER

2 OZ
VODKA

.5 OZ
LIME JUICE

TRY IT IN A LOWBALL GLASS (OR A COPPER MUG).

FIRST THINGS FIRST, GO BUY SOME:

■ DUBONNET ROUGE

OH, AND MAKE SURE YOU HAVE A LEMON TOO

> REPORTEDLY QUEEN ELIZABETH II'S FAVORITE MORNING
> COCKTAIL. YEP, SHE PREGAMES HER LUNCH.

INGREDIENTS	INSTRUCTIONS
1.5 OZ DRY GIN	GET MIXING GLASS ☐
1.5 OZ DUBONNET ROUGE	FILL WITH ICE ☐
1 DASH ORANGE BITTERS	ADD ALL INGREDIENTS ☐
LEMON (GARNISH)	STIR UNTIL CHILLED ☐
	STRAIN INTO SERVING GLASS ☐
	GARNISH W/ LEMON TWIST ☐

WHAT DO YOU THINK?

. . . .

. . . .

. . . .

. . . .

DRINK THIS AGAIN?   YES ☐   NO ☐   IF DESPERATE ☐

BONUS TRIVIA

HERE IS THE QUEEN'S PREFERRED RECIPE: 2 PARTS DUBONNET
ROUGE, ONE PART GORDON'S GIN, A SLICE OF LEMON, AND
EXACTLY TWO CUBES OF ICE.

1.5 OZ
DRY GIN

1.5 OZ
DUBONNET
ROUGE

1 DASH
ORANGE BITTERS

WE BET THE QUEEN USES A COUPE, YOU PEASANT.

YOU PRETTY MUCH HAVE EVERYTHING YOU NEED:

- JUST MAKE SURE YOU HAVE SOME SUGAR (AND SALT)

OH. AND YOU'LL ALSO NEED A GRAPEFRUIT

SUPPOSEDLY THIS IS A DWAYNE JOHNSON FAVORITE. WE ARE BETTING SOMEONE MAKES THEM FOR HIM, THOUGH.

INGREDIENTS

- 2 OZ GRAPEFRUIT JUICE
- 1 TBSP LIME JUICE
- 1 TSP SUGAR
- 2 OZ BLANCO TEQUILA
- 2 OZ CLUB SODA
- SALT (RIM OF GLASS)
- GRAPEFRUIT (GARNISH)

INSTRUCTIONS

GET SERVING GLASS ☐
RIM W/ GRAPEFRUIT JUICE ☐
DIP IN SALT ☐
ADD FIRST 2 INGREDIENTS ☐
STIR IN SUGAR ☐
FILL WITH ICE ☐
POUR IN TEQUILA ☐
TOP WITH CLUB SODA ☐
GARNISH W/ GRAPEFRUIT WEDGE ☐

WHAT DO YOU THINK?

. . . .

DRINK THIS AGAIN?   YES ☐   NO ☐   IF DESPERATE ☐

BONUS TRIVIA

LIKELY NAMED AFTER 'LA PALOMA,' A POPULAR FOLK SONG
FROM THE 1860s THAT'S BEEN RECORDED OVER 1,000 TIMES.

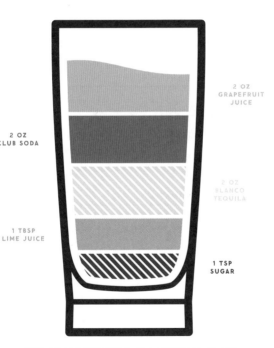

2 OZ
GRAPEFRUIT
JUICE

2 OZ
CLUB SODA

2 OZ
BLANCO
TEQUILA

1 TBSP
LIME JUICE

1 TSP
SUGAR

THIS ONE LOOKS GREAT IN A HIGHBALL GLASS.

YOU SHOULD HAVE EVERYTHING YOU NEED:

█ SO MAYBE MAKE SOME NACHOS OR SOMETHING

CHECK YOUR BAR FOR ANYTHING YOU'RE GETTING LOW ON, THOUGH

TEQUILA DOESN'T ACTUALLY HAVE A WORM IN IT.
YOU'RE THINKING OF MEZCAL.

INGREDIENTS	INSTRUCTIONS
3 OZ PINEAPPLE JUICE	GET SHAKER & ADD ICE ☐
2 OZ BLANCO TEQUILA	ADD ALL INGREDIENTS ☐
.5 OZ LIME JUICE	SHAKE UNTIL CHILLED ☐
	FILL SERVING GLASS W/ ICE ☐
	STRAIN INTO GLASS ☐

WHAT DO YOU THINK?

. . . .

. . . .

. . . .

. . . .

DRINK THIS AGAIN?   YES ☐   NO ☐   IF DESPERATE ☐

BONUS TRIVIA

BULLFIGHTING, WHILE THANKFULLY ILLEGAL IN MOST OF THE
WORLD, IS STILL PRACTICED IN PARTS OF PORTUGAL AND SPAIN.

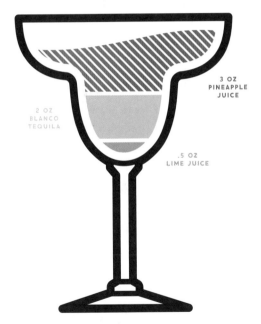

3 OZ
PINEAPPLE
JUICE

2 OZ
BLANCO
TEQUILA

.5 OZ
LIME JUICE

THE PERFECT EXCUSE TO BUY A MARGARITA GLASS.

YOU SHOULD HAVE EVERYTHING YOU NEED:

JUST MAKE SURE YOU HAVE A LEMON

AND MAYBE GIVE YOUR PARENTS A CALL. THEY'D LIKE THAT

THIS DRINK HAS ABOUT AS MUCH TO DO WITH JAPAN
AS FRENCH FRIES HAVE TO DO WITH FRANCE.

INGREDIENTS	INSTRUCTIONS
2 OZ COGNAC	GET SHAKER & ADD ICE ☐
.5 OZ ORGEAT	ADD ALL INGREDIENTS ☐
2 DASH ANGOSTURA BITTERS	SHAKE UNTIL CHILLED ☐
LEMON (GARNISH)	STRAIN INTO GLASS ☐
	GARNISH W/ LEMON TWIST ☐

WHAT DO YOU THINK?

. . . .

. . . .

. . . .

DRINK THIS AGAIN?   YES ☐   NO ☐   IF DESPERATE ☐

BONUS TRIVIA

THE WORLD'S SHORTEST ESCALATOR IS IN THE BASEMENT
OF MORE'S DEPARTMENT STORE IN KAWASAKI, JAPAN. IT HAS
ONLY 5 STEPS AND IS 33 INCHES HIGH.

2 OZ
COGNAC

2 DASH
ANGOSTURA
BITTERS

5 OZ
ORGEAT

USE A COUPE GLASS. TRUST US, IT'S WORTH IT.

FIRST THINGS FIRST, GO BUY SOME:

PEACH LIQUEUR

OH, AND YOU'LL ALSO NEED AN ORANGE

PROSECCO SHOULD BE SERVED CHILLED, BUT DON'T STORE IT IN THE FRIDGE FOR MORE THAN 3 DAYS.

INGREDIENTS	INSTRUCTIONS
.5 OZ ANISETTE LIQUEUR	GET SERVING GLASS ☐
1.5 OZ PEACH LIQUEUR	ADD FIRST 2 INGREDIENTS ☐
PROSECCO	TOP WITH PROSECCO ☐
ORANGE (GARNISH)	GARNISH W/ ORANGE TWIST ☐

WHAT DO YOU THINK?

. . . .

. . . .

. . . .

. . . .

. . . .

. . . .

DRINK THIS AGAIN?   YES ☐   NO ☐   IF DESPERATE ☐

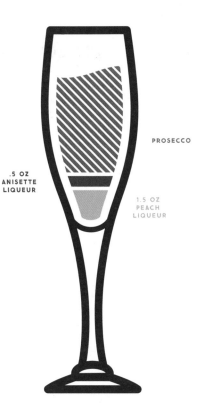

PROSECCO

.5 OZ
ANISETTE
LIQUEUR

1.5 OZ
PEACH
LIQUEUR

FINALLY, A USE FOR THOSE CHAMPAGNE FLUTES.

YOU PRETTY MUCH HAVE EVERYTHING YOU NEED:

JUST CHECK THE FRESHNESS OF THOSE JUICES

OH, AND YOU'LL ALSO NEED A LEMON

ONE THIRD OF ALL CHAMPAGNE SALES HAPPEN DURING THE MONTHS OF NOVEMBER AND DECEMBER.

INGREDIENTS

.75 OZ MARASCHINO LIQUEUR
1 OZ PINEAPPLE JUICE
1 OZ ORANGE JUICE
4 OZ CHAMPAGNE
LEMON (GARNISH)

INSTRUCTIONS

GET MIXING GLASS ☐
FILL WITH ICE ☐
ADD FIRST 3 INGREDIENTS ☐
POUR IN CHAMPAGNE ☐
STIR GENTLY ☐
STRAIN INTO SERVING GLASS ☐
GARNISH W/ LEMON PEEL ☐

WHAT DO YOU THINK?

. . . .

. . . .

DRINK THIS AGAIN?   YES ☐   NO ☐   IF DESPERATE ☐

4 OZ
CHAMPAGNE

1 OZ ORANGE
JUICE

.75 OZ
MARASCHINO
LIQUEUR

1 OZ
PINEAPPLE
JUICE

GET THAT CHAMPAGNE FLUTE OUT OF THE DISHWASHER.

FIRST THINGS FIRST, GO BUY SOME:

APPLE JUICE

JUST MAKE SURE YOU HAVE A RASPBERRY (AND SOME MINT)

NAMED AFTER A HISTORIC INTERSECTION IN THE WEST
END OF LONDON WHERE 7 STREETS CONVERGE.

INGREDIENTS

INSTRUCTIONS

INGREDIENTS	INSTRUCTIONS
1.25 OZ APPLE JUICE	GET SHAKER & ADD ICE ☐
.5 OZ LIME JUICE	ADD FIRST 6 INGREDIENTS ☐
.25 OZ CAMPARI	SHAKE UNTIL CHILLED ☐
.25 OZ GRENADINE	STRAIN INTO GLASS ☐
.75 OZ DRY GIN	TOP WITH CHAMPAGNE ☐
.25 OZ SIMPLE SYRUP	GARNISH W/ RASPBERRY ☐
CHAMPAGNE	ADD MINT LEAF ☐
RASPBERRY (GARNISH)	
MINT LEAF (GARNISH)	

WHAT DO YOU THINK?

. . . .

DRINK THIS AGAIN?   YES ☐   NO ☐   IF DESPERATE ☐

BONUS TRIVIA

THE SEVEN DIALS JUNCTION HAS A COLUMN WITH 6 SUNDIALS.
IT WAS COMMISSIONED BEFORE A 7TH STREET WAS ADDED.

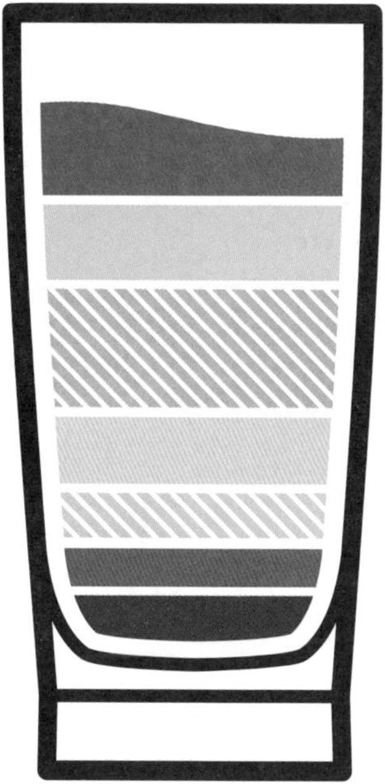

CHAMPAGNE

.75 OZ
DRY GIN

1.25 OZ
APPLE
JUICE

.5 OZ
LIME JUICE

.25 OZ
CAMPARI

.25 OZ
GRENADINE

.25 OZ
SIMPLE
SYRUP

YOU SHOULD PROBABLY USE A HIGHBALL GLASS.

FIRST THINGS FIRST, GO BUY SOME:

▪ BRANDY

OH, AND YOU'LL ALSO NEED SOME SUGAR (AND A LEMON)

> THE WORD BRANDY IS DERIVED FROM THE DUTCH WORD
> BRANDEWIJN, WHICH TRANSLATES TO 'BURNT WINE.'

INGREDIENTS	INSTRUCTIONS
2 OZ BRANDY	RUB GLASS RIM W/ LEMON ☐
1 DASH TRIPLE SEC	DIP IN SUGAR ☐
1 DASH ANGOSTURA BITTERS	GET SHAKER & ADD ICE ☐
1 OZ CHAMPAGNE	ADD FIRST 3 INGREDIENTS ☐
SUGAR (RIM OF GLASS)	SHAKE UNTIL CHILLED ☐
LEMON (GARNISH)	FILL RIMMED GLASS W/ ICE ☐
	STRAIN INTO GLASS ☐
	TOP WITH CHAMPAGNE ☐
	GARNISH W/ LEMON TWIST ☐

WHAT DO YOU THINK?

. . . .

DRINK THIS AGAIN?   YES ☐   NO ☐   IF DESPERATE ☐

BONUS TRIVIA

THE CHICAGO RIVER IS THE ONLY ONE IN THE WORLD THAT CURRENTLY FLOWS BACKWARDS.

DUE TO SOME SANITARY CONCERNS IN THE LATE 1800s (AKA: SEWAGE FLOWING UPSTREAM INTO THE DRINKING WATER SUPPLY), THE CITY USED A SERIES OF LOCKS AND CANALS TO PERMANENTLY REVERSE THE COURSE OF THE RIVER.

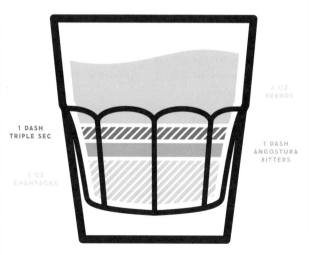

2 OZ BRANDY

1 DASH TRIPLE SEC

1 DASH ANGOSTURA BITTERS

1 OZ CHAMPAGNE

WE'D RECOMMEND A LOWBALL GLASS FOR THIS ONE.

YOU PRETTY MUCH HAVE EVERYTHING YOU NEED:

■ JUST MAKE SURE YOU HAVE AN EXTRA LIME

CHECK YOUR BAR FOR ANYTHING YOU'RE GETTING LOW ON. THOUGH

CREATED IN THE 1920s AS THE SIGNATURE DRINK OF THE
'PEGU CLUB,' A GENTLEMAN'S CLUB IN YANGON, MYANMAR.

INGREDIENTS   INSTRUCTIONS

■ 2 OZ DRY GIN   GET SHAKER & ADD ICE ☐
■ .75 OZ TRIPLE SEC   ADD ALL INGREDIENTS ☐
■ .75 OZ LIME JUICE   SHAKE UNTIL CHILLED ☐
■ 1 DASH ANGOSTURA BITTERS   STRAIN INTO GLASS ☐
■ 1 DASH ORANGE BITTERS   GARNISH W/ LIME SLICE ☐
■ LIME (GARNISH)

WHAT DO YOU THINK?

. . . .

. . . .

. . . .

DRINK THIS AGAIN?   YES ☐   NO ☐   IF DESPERATE ☐

BONUS TRIVIA

WE OWE ITS RESURGENCE TO AUDREY SAUNDERS, WHO OPENED HER 'PEGU CLUB' IN NYC (UNTIL COVID SADLY CLOSED IT).

.75 OZ
TRIPLE SEC

1 DASH
ANGOSTURA
BITTERS

2 OZ
DRY GIN

1 DASH
ORANGE
BITTERS

.75 OZ
LIME JUICE

THIS ONE DEFINITELY CALLS FOR A MARTINI GLASS.

YOU PRETTY MUCH HAVE EVERYTHING YOU NEED:

☐ JUST CHECK THE FRESHNESS OF THOSE JUICES

YOU'LL ALSO NEED CARDAMOM PODS (BUT WHO DOESN'T HAVE THOSE?)

> CARDAMOM IS THE SECOND MOST EXPENSIVE SPICE IN THE WORLD. ONLY SAFFRON IS PRICIER. SORRY.

INGREDIENTS

- 2 OZ DRY GIN
- 1 OZ PINEAPPLE JUICE
- .75 OZ LIME JUICE
- .75 OZ SIMPLE SYRUP
- 3 CARDAMOM PODS
- TONIC WATER

INSTRUCTIONS

- GET SHAKER ☐
- MUDDLE CARDAMOM PODS ☐
- FILL WITH ICE ☐
- ADD FIRST 4 INGREDIENTS ☐
- SHAKE UNTIL CHILLED ☐
- FILL SERVING GLASS W/ ICE ☐
- STRAIN INTO GLASS ☐
- TOP W/ TONIC WATER ☐

WHAT DO YOU THINK?

. . . .

. . . .

DRINK THIS AGAIN?　YES ☐　NO ☐　IF DESPERATE ☐

BONUS TRIVIA

THIS DRINK IS LIKELY THE NAMESAKE OF THE 1890 POEM BY RUDYARD KIPLING. IT'S BEST REMEMBERED FOR ITS FINAL LINE: 'YOU'RE A BETTER MAN THAN I AM, GUNGA DIN.'

BONUS BONUS TRIVIA: WHILE 'DIN' IS USUALLY PRONOUNCED AS IF IT RHYMES WITH 'PIN,' THE LINES OF THE POEM MAKE IT CLEAR THAT IT SHOULD RHYME WITH 'GREEN.'

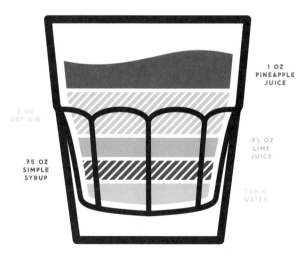

1 OZ
PINEAPPLE
JUICE

2 OZ
DRY GIN

.75 OZ
LIME
JUICE

.75 OZ
SIMPLE
SYRUP

TONIC
WATER

WE'D RECOMMEND A LOWBALL GLASS FOR THIS ONE.

FIRST THINGS FIRST, GO BUY SOME:

▨ BOURBON

OH, AND YOU'LL ALSO NEED AN ORANGE (AND SOME SUGAR)

SERVED IN THE 1961 FILM 'BREAKFAST AT TIFFANY'S.' THE DRINK HOLDS UP. MICKEY ROONEY CERTAINLY DOESN'T.

INGREDIENTS   **INSTRUCTIONS**

▨ 2 OZ COGNAC   GET SHAKER & ADD ICE ☐
▨ 1 OZ BOURBON   ADD ALL INGREDIENTS ☐
▨ 1 OZ DARK RUM   SHAKE UNTIL CHILLED ☐
▨ .5 OZ LEMON JUICE   GET SERVING GLASS ☐
▨ 2 TSP SUGAR   FILL WITH ICE ☐
▨ ORANGE (GARNISH)   STRAIN INTO GLASS ☐
                                    GARNISH W/ ORANGE SLICE ☐

WHAT DO YOU THINK?

. . . .

. . . .

DRINK THIS AGAIN?   YES ☐   NO ☐   IF DESPERATE ☐

MAKE A MISSISSIPPI PUNCH

BONUS TRIVIA

PETAL, MISSISSIPPI, IS HOME TO THE INTERNATIONAL CHECKERS HALL OF FAME. SOMEONE, PLEASE TAKE A PHOTO FOR US.

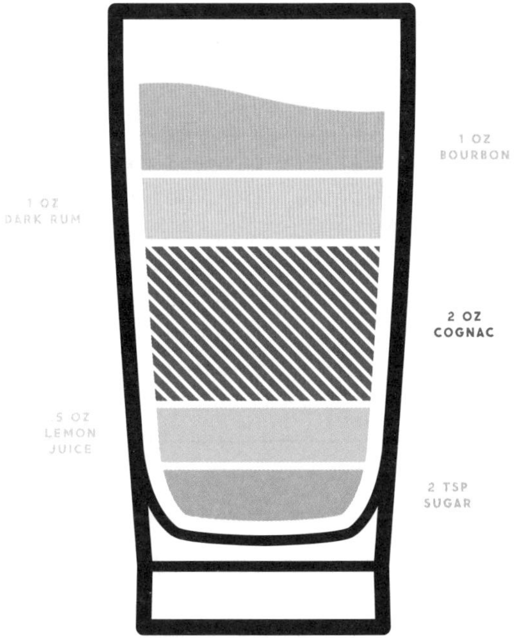

1 OZ
BOURBON
1 OZ
DARK RUM
2 OZ
COGNAC
.5 OZ
LEMON
JUICE
2 TSP
SUGAR

YOU SHOULD PROBABLY USE A HIGHBALL GLASS.

YOU PRETTY MUCH HAVE EVERYTHING YOU NEED:

☐ JUST MAKE SURE YOU HAVE A LEMON

CHECK YOUR BAR FOR ANYTHING YOU'RE GETTING LOW ON, THOUGH

THIS DRINK WAS CREATED BY HARRY MACELHONE AT
'HARRY'S NEW YORK BAR' IN PARIS, FRANCE.

INGREDIENTS

INSTRUCTIONS

INGREDIENTS	INSTRUCTIONS	
1.5 OZ BOURBON	CHILL SERVING GLASS	☐
.75 OZ DRY VERMOUTH	GET MIXING GLASS	☐
.75 OZ CAMPARI	FILL WITH ICE	☐
LEMON (GARNISH)	ADD ALL INGREDIENTS	☐
	STIR UNTIL CHILLED	☐
	STRAIN INTO SERVING GLASS	☐
	GARNISH W/ LEMON TWIST	☐

WHAT DO YOU THINK?

. . . .

. . . .

DRINK THIS AGAIN?　　YES ☐　　NO ☐　　IF DESPERATE ☐

SPORTS JOURNALIST WILLIAM ROBERTSON, A REGULAR AT
HARRY'S BAR IN THE 1920s, INSPIRED THE NAME FOR THIS
COCKTAIL. WILLIAM CALLED EVERYONE 'OLD PAL.'

1.5 OZ
BOURBON

.75 OZ
DRY
VERMOUTH

.75 OZ
CAMPARI

USE A COUPE GLASS. TRUST US, IT'S WORTH IT.

YOU PRETTY MUCH HAVE EVERYTHING YOU NEED:

☐ JUST MAKE SURE YOU HAVE SOME SUGAR

OH, AND YOU'LL ALSO NEED A LEMON (IMAGINE THAT)

THIS IS SUPPOSEDLY ONE OF OPRAH'S FAVORITE
COCKTAILS, BUT WE HAVEN'T TALKED TO HER LATELY.

INGREDIENTS

- 2 OZ VODKA
- .5 OZ TRIPLE SEC
- 1 OZ LEMON JUICE
- 1 OZ SIMPLE SYRUP
- SUGAR (RIM OF GLASS)
- LEMON (GARNISH)

INSTRUCTIONS

GET SERVING GLASS ☐
RIM W/ LEMON JUICE ☐
DIP IN SUGAR ☐
GET SHAKER & ADD ICE ☐
ADD ALL INGREDIENTS ☐
SHAKE UNTIL CHILLED ☐
STRAIN INTO GLASS ☐
GARNISH W/ LEMON TWIST ☐

WHAT DO YOU THINK?

. . . .

. . . .

DRINK THIS AGAIN?   YES ☐   NO ☐   IF DESPERATE ☐

BONUS TRIVIA

CREATED IN THE 1970s AT 'HENRY AFRICA'S' IN SAN FRANCISCO, CALIFORNIA. SORRY, IT CLOSED IN 1986. YOU JUST MISSED IT.

1 OZ
LEMON
JUICE

1 OZ
SIMPLE
SYRUP

2 OZ
VODKA

.5 OZ
TRIPLE SEC

THIS ONE LOOKS GREAT IN A MARTINI GLASS.

FIRST THINGS FIRST, GO BUY SOME:

PEYCHAUD'S BITTERS

OH, AND YOU'LL ALSO NEED A LEMON

IT WAS ORIGINALLY CLAIMED TO BE A LOST CLASSIC
OF THE SEELBACH HOTEL...BUT IT WAS ALL FAKE.*

INGREDIENTS	INSTRUCTIONS
1 OZ BOURBON	CHILL CHAMPAGNE ☐
.5 OZ TRIPLE SEC	GET SERVING GLASS ☐
7 DASH ANGOSTURA BITTERS	ADD FIRST 4 LIQUIDS ☐
7 DASH PEYCHAUD'S BITTERS	STIR TO COMBINE ☐
CHAMPAGNE	TOP WITH CHAMPAGNE ☐
LEMON (GARNISH)	GARNISH W/ LEMON TWIST ☐

WHAT DO YOU THINK?

. . . .

. . . .

. . . .

*SERIOUSLY, YOU SHOULD LOOK THIS ONE UP. IT'S WORTH THE READ.

DRINK THIS AGAIN?　　　YES ☐　　NO ☐　　IF DESPERATE ☐

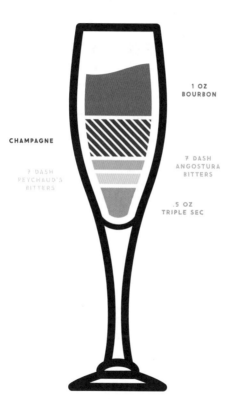

1 OZ
BOURBON

CHAMPAGNE

7 DASH
PEYCHAUD'S
BITTERS

7 DASH
ANGOSTURA
BITTERS

.5 OZ
TRIPLE SEC

FINALLY, A USE FOR THOSE CHAMPAGNE FLUTES.

YOU PRETTY MUCH HAVE EVERYTHING YOU NEED:

■ JUST MAKE SURE YOU HAVE VANILLA ICE CREAM

CHECK YOUR BAR FOR ANYTHING YOU'RE GETTING LOW ON, THOUGH

CREATED IN 1968 BY JEROME ADAMS AT THE 'BAYVIEW
YACHT CLUB' IN DETROIT, MICHIGAN.

INGREDIENTS	INSTRUCTIONS
2 SCOOPS VANILLA ICE CREAM	GET BLENDER ☐
1.5 OZ WHITE RUM	ADD 3-5 ICE CUBES ☐
1.5 OZ COFFEE LIQUEUR	ADD ALL INGREDIENTS ☐
	BLEND UNTIL SMOOTH ☐
	POUR INTO SERVING GLASS ☐

WHAT DO YOU THINK?

. . . .

. . . .

. . . .

. . . .

DRINK THIS AGAIN?   YES ☐   NO ☐   IF DESPERATE ☐

BONUS TRIVIA

AN EARLY PATRON SAID THAT THE THEN-UNNAMED DRINK 'KIND OF MAKES YOU WANT TO HUM.' SUDDENLY, IT HAD A NAME.

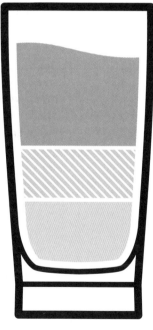

2 SCOOPS
VANILLA
ICE CREAM

1.5 OZ
COFFEE
LIQUEUR

1.5 OZ
WHITE RUM

YOU SHOULD PROBABLY USE A HIGHBALL GLASS.

YOU PRETTY MUCH HAVE EVERYTHING YOU NEED:

JUST MAKE SURE YOU HAVE AN ORANGE AROUND

AND MAYBE CHECK THE FRESHNESS OF THAT LIME JUICE

ONE OF THE FEW CASES WHERE THE SEQUEL IS
ACTUALLY BETTER THAN THE ORIGINAL.

INGREDIENTS	INSTRUCTIONS
1 OZ DRY GIN	CHILL SERVING GLASS ☐
1 OZ LILLET BLANC	GET SHAKER & ADD ICE ☐
1 OZ TRIPLE SEC	ADD ALL INGREDIENTS ☐
1 OZ LEMON JUICE	SHAKE UNTIL CHILLED ☐
1 DASH ABSINTHE	STRAIN INTO SERVING GLASS ☐
ORANGE (GARNISH)	GARNISH W/ ORANGE TWIST ☐

WHAT DO YOU THINK?

. . . .

. . . .

. . . .

. . . .

DRINK THIS AGAIN?   YES ☐   NO ☐   IF DESPERATE ☐

BONUS TRIVIA

DURING THE LATE 1800s, THE TERM 'CORPSE REVIVER' WAS
USED TO DESCRIBE AN ENTIRE CATEGORY OF COCKTAILS THAT
WERE CREATED TO BE HANGOVER CURES.

1 OZ
DRY GIN

1 OZ
LILLET
BLANC

1 OZ
TRIPLE
SEC

1 OZ
LEMON
JUICE

1 DASH
ABSINTHE

USE A COUPE GLASS. TRUST US, IT'S WORTH IT.

FIRST THINGS FIRST, GO BUY SOME:

■ SCOTCH

OH, AND YOU'LL ALSO NEED TO HAVE A LIME

NAMED AFTER THE LATE 1800s BROADWAY STAR
MAYME TAYLOR. YEP, THEY MISSPELLED HER NAME.

INGREDIENTS   **INSTRUCTIONS**

■ 2 OZ SCOTCH   GET SERVING GLASS ☐
■ .5 OZ LIME JUICE   FILL WITH ICE ☐
■ 5 OZ GINGER BEER   ADD FIRST 2 INGREDIENTS ☐
■ LIME (GARNISH)   TOP WITH GINGER BEER ☐
                             GARNISH W/ LIME WEDGE ☐

WHAT DO YOU THINK?

. . . .

. . . .

. . . .

DRINK THIS AGAIN?   YES ☐   NO ☐   IF DESPERATE ☐

AFTER A CRUISE ON LAKE ONTARIO IN 1899, MAYME ORDERED A
CLARET LEMONADE. THEY WERE OUT & MADE THIS INSTEAD.

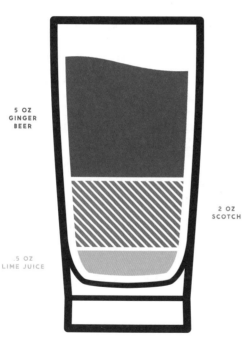

5 OZ
GINGER
BEER

2 OZ
SCOTCH

.5 OZ
LIME JUICE

YOU SHOULD PROBABLY USE A HIGHBALL GLASS.

YOU PRETTY MUCH HAVE EVERYTHING YOU NEED:

JUST MAKE SURE THAT YOU STILL HAVE SUGAR CUBES

OH, AND YOU'LL NEED A LEMON TOO

NAMED AFTER THE SAZERAC BRAND COGNAC THAT WAS USED IN THE ORIGINAL (INSTEAD OF WHISKEY).

INGREDIENTS	INSTRUCTIONS
2 DASH PEYCHAUD'S BITTERS	GET MIXING GLASS ☐
1 DASH ANGOSTURA BITTERS	ADD SUGAR CUBE ☐
1.5 OZ RYE WHISKEY	ADD BITTERS & WATER ☐
.25 OZ ABSINTHE	MUDDLE & FILL W/ ICE ☐
1 SUGAR CUBE	ADD WHISKEY & STIR ☐
.5 TSP WATER	GET SERVING GLASS ☐
LEMON (GARNISH)	COAT INSIDE W/ ABSINTHE ☐
	STRAIN INTO GLASS OVER ICE ☐
	GARNISH W/ LEMON TWIST ☐

WHAT DO YOU THINK?

. . . .

DRINK THIS AGAIN?   YES ☐   NO ☐   IF DESPERATE ☐

BONUS TRIVIA

MANY CLAIM THAT ANTOINE PEYCHAUD INVENTED THE SAZERAC
IN HIS PHARMACY AT 437 ROYAL STREET IN NEW ORLEANS, LA.

THERE HE WOULD SERVE THEM IN AN EGG-SHAPED GLASS
CALLED A COQUETIER (PRONOUNCED COOK-TEE), WHICH SOME
SAY IS THE ORIGIN OF THE WORD 'COCKTAIL.'

IS ALL OF THIS TRUE? WHO KNOWS, EVERYONE WAS DRUNK.

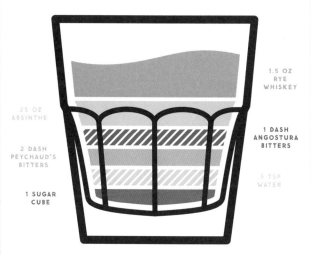

.25 OZ
ABSINTHE

2 DASH
PEYCHAUD'S
BITTERS

1 SUGAR
CUBE

1.5 OZ
RYE
WHISKEY

1 DASH
ANGOSTURA
BITTERS

5 TSP
WATER

WE'D RECOMMEND A LOWBALL GLASS FOR THIS ONE.

YOU PRETTY MUCH HAVE EVERYTHING YOU NEED:

■ SO MAKE A DRINK ALREADY

CHECK YOUR BAR FOR ANYTHING YOU'RE GETTING LOW ON, THOUGH

THE LEAST FREQUENTLY USED LETTER IN THE ENGLISH
LANGUAGE IS Z. THE MOST FREQUENT? E.

INGREDIENTS

1 OZ WHITE RUM	GET SHAKER & ADD ICE ☐
.5 OZ LEMON JUICE	ADD ALL INGREDIENTS ☐
.5 OZ TRIPLE SEC	SHAKE UNTIL CHILLED ☐
	STRAIN INTO GLASS ☐

INSTRUCTIONS

WHAT DO YOU THINK?

. . . .

. . . .

. . . .

. . . .

. . . .

DRINK THIS AGAIN?   YES ☐   NO ☐   IF DESPERATE ☐

BONUS TRIVIA

'PACK MY BOX WITH FIVE DOZEN LIQUOR JUGS' USES ALL 26
LETTERS OF THE ALPHABET. THAT'S CALLED A PANGRAM.

1 OZ
WHITE
RUM

.5 OZ
LEMON JUICE

.5 OZ
TRIPLE SEC

THIS ONE DEFINITELY CALLS FOR A MARTINI GLASS.

MAKE A HOLLAND HOUSE 99

YOU PRETTY MUCH HAVE EVERYTHING YOU NEED:

■ JUST MAKE SURE YOU HAVE A LEMON

AND MAYBE CHECK THE FRESHNESS OF THAT JUICE

THE SIGNATURE COCKTAIL OF THE 'HOLLAND HOUSE
HOTEL' IN NYC (WELL, PRE-PROHIBITION ANYWAY).

INGREDIENTS

- 1.75 OZ GENEVER GIN
- .25 OZ MARASCHINO LIQUEUR
- .5 OZ LEMON JUICE
- .75 OZ DRY VERMOUTH
- LEMON (GARNISH)

INSTRUCTIONS

- GET SHAKER ☐
- FILL WITH ICE ☐
- ADD ALL INGREDIENTS ☐
- SHAKE UNTIL CHILLED ☐
- STRAIN INTO GLASS ☐
- GARNISH W/ LEMON TWIST ☐

WHAT DO YOU THINK?

. . . .

. . . .

. . . .

DRINK THIS AGAIN?   YES ☐   NO ☐   IF DESPERATE ☐

BONUS TRIVIA

DESPITE BEING USED INTERCHANGEABLY, THE NETHERLANDS IS
THE CORRECT TERM FOR THE COUNTRY AS A WHOLE (WITH
ALL TWELVE PROVINCES), WHILE HOLLAND REFERS TO JUST
TWO OF THEM (NORTH AND SOUTH HOLLAND).

1.75 OZ
GENEVER
GIN

.25 OZ
MARASCHINO
LIQUEUR

.75 OZ
DRY
VERMOUTH

.5 OZ
LEMON JUICE

IF IT WERE US, WE'D GO WITH A COUPE GLASS.

FIRST THINGS FIRST, GO BUY SOME:

CRANBERRY JUICE

OH, AND YOU'LL ALSO NEED A LIME

IT'S RUMORED TO BE A PERSONAL FAVORITE OF RENEE ZELLWEGER, IF THAT DOES ANYTHING FOR YOU.

INGREDIENTS

2 OZ VODKA
1 OZ LILLET BLANC
3 OZ CRANBERRY JUICE
1 SPLASH LIME JUICE
LIME (GARNISH)

INSTRUCTIONS

CHILL SERVING GLASS ☐
GET SHAKER & ADD ICE ☐
ADD FIRST 3 INGREDIENTS ☐
SHAKE UNTIL CHILLED ☐
STRAIN INTO GLASS ☐
ADD SPLASH OF LIME JUICE ☐
GARNISH W/ LIME WEDGE ☐

WHAT DO YOU THINK?

. . . .

. . . .

. . . .

DRINK THIS AGAIN?   YES ☐   NO ☐   IF DESPERATE ☐

TRY PAIRING IT WITH THE 1978 ALBUM OF THE SAME NAME BY
FRENCH JAZZ FUSION ARTIST JEAN-LUC PONTY. WE DIDN'T.

2 OZ
VODKA

1 OZ
LILLET BLANC

3 OZ
CRANBERRY
JUICE

1 SPLASH
LIME JUICE

THIS ONE DEFINITELY CALLS FOR A MARTINI GLASS.

YOU PRETTY MUCH HAVE EVERYTHING YOU NEED:

JUST MAKE SURE THAT YOU HAVE AN ORANGE

CHECK YOUR BAR FOR ANYTHING YOU'RE GETTING LOW ON, THOUGH

DURING THE SUMMER, THE EIFFEL TOWER IS ABOUT 6"
TALLER DUE TO THE EXPANSION OF METAL IN THE HEAT.

INGREDIENTS	INSTRUCTIONS
1 OZ ORANGE LIQUEUR	GET SERVING GLASS ☐
2 OZ BOURBON	ADD ORANGE SLICE ☐
2 OZ GINGER ALE	POUR IN ORANGE LIQUEUR ☐
ORANGE SLICE	MUDDLE UNTIL MIXED ☐
	FILL WITH ICE ☐
	ADD REMAINING INGREDIENTS ☐
	STIR UNTIL CHILLED ☐

WHAT DO YOU THINK?

. . . .

. . . .

DRINK THIS AGAIN? YES ☐ NO ☐ IF DESPERATE ☐

BONUS TRIVIA

THE BEAUFORT SCALE OF WIND INCLUDES 5 DIFFERENT BREEZE
STRENGTHS: LIGHT, GENTLE, MODERATE, FRESH, AND STRONG.

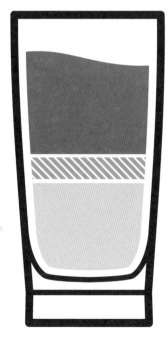

2 OZ
BOURBON

1 OZ
ORANGE
LIQUEUR

2 OZ
GINGER ALE

YOU SHOULD PROBABLY USE A HIGHBALL GLASS.

YOU PRETTY MUCH HAVE EVERYTHING YOU NEED:

JUST MAKE SURE YOU HAVE A PINEAPPLE

OH, AND A BRANDIED CHERRY WOULD BE NICE TOO.

WHAT WE KNOW: THIS DRINK WAS CREATED IN SEATTLE.
WHAT WE DON'T KNOW: LITERALLY EVERYTHING ELSE.

INGREDIENTS

- 1 OZ WHITE RUM
- 1 OZ VODKA
- 1.5 OZ PINEAPPLE JUICE
- .5 OZ LEMON JUICE
- .25 OZ SIMPLE SYRUP
- BRANDIED CHERRY (GARNISH)
- PINEAPPLE (GARNISH)

INSTRUCTIONS

- GET BLENDER ☐
- FILL W/ 6 OZ OF ICE ☐
- ADD ALL INGREDIENTS ☐
- BLEND UNTIL SMOOTH ☐
- POUR INTO GLASS ☐
- GARNISH W/ CHERRY ☐
- ADD PINEAPPLE WEDGE ☐

WHAT DO YOU THINK?

. . . .

. . . .

DRINK THIS AGAIN?   YES ☐   NO ☐   IF DESPERATE ☐

THE TERM 'TABOO' WAS INTRODUCED INTO ENGLISH BY CAPTAIN
COOK IN 1771, ORIGINATING FROM THE TONGAN WORD 'TABU.'

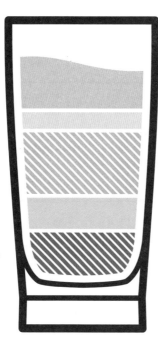

1 OZ
WHITE RUM

.25 OZ
SIMPLE
SYRUP

1.5 OZ
PINEAPPLE
JUICE

.5 OZ
LEMON
JUICE

1 OZ
VODKA

TRY A HIGHBALL GLASS (OR USE A TIKI MUG).

YOU PRETTY MUCH HAVE EVERYTHING YOU NEED:

JUST MAKE SURE YOU HAVE AN EXTRA LEMON

AND MAYBE CHECK THE FRESHNESS OF THAT JUICE

WHEN USED IN COCKTAILS, JASMINE PROVIDES STRONG FLORAL FLAVORS. THIS DRINK DOESN'T USE ANY.

INGREDIENTS	INSTRUCTIONS
1.5 OZ DRY GIN	GET SHAKER & ADD ICE ☐
.75 OZ LEMON JUICE	ADD ALL INGREDIENTS ☐
.25 OZ CAMPARI	SHAKE UNTIL CHILLED ☐
.25 OZ TRIPLE SEC	STRAIN INTO SERVING GLASS ☐
LEMON (GARNISH)	GARNISH W/ LEMON TWIST ☐

WHAT DO YOU THINK?

. . . .

. . . .

. . . .

. . . .

DRINK THIS AGAIN?   YES ☐   NO ☐   IF DESPERATE ☐

BONUS TRIVIA

PAUL HARRINGTON MADE UP THIS DRINK FOR MATT JASMIN, A
FRIEND THAT HE WENT TO SCHOOL WITH. WHEN HE LATER PUT IT
ON THE MENUS, HE ACCIDENTALLY SPELLED HIS NAME WRONG.

.75 OZ
LEMON
JUICE

.25 OZ
TRIPLE
SEC

.25 OZ
CAMPARI

1.5 OZ
DRY GIN

USE A COUPE GLASS. TRUST US, IT'S WORTH IT.

FIRST THINGS FIRST, GO BUY SOME:

- SOUR MIX

OH, AND YOU'LL ALSO NEED A SPRIG OF MINT

THE INTERNET SAYS THAT GEORGE CLOONEY LOVES THIS ONE, BUT WE DON'T BELIEVE IT. EMAIL US, GEORGE.*

INGREDIENTS

- 2 OZ VODKA
- 2 OZ RASPBERRY LIQUEUR
- 2 OZ CREAM
- 1 OZ SOUR MIX
- MINT SPRIG (GARNISH)

INSTRUCTIONS

- GET SHAKER & ADD ICE ☐
- ADD ALL INGREDIENTS ☐
- SHAKE UNTIL CHILLED ☐
- STRAIN INTO SERVING GLASS ☐
- GARNISH W/ MINT SPRIG ☐

WHAT DO YOU THINK?

. . . .

. . . .

. . . .

. . . .

*THISISONLYFORGEORGECLOONEY@BRASSMONKEYGOODS.COM

DRINK THIS AGAIN?   YES ☐   NO ☐   IF DESPERATE ☐

BONUS TRIVIA

MADE AT THE 'CHERRY NIGHTCLUB' INSIDE OF THE RED ROCKS
CASINO IN LAS VEGAS, NV (UNTIL IT CLOSED IN 2010).

2 OZ
VODKA

2 OZ
CREAM

2 OZ
RASPBERRY
LIQUEUR

1 OZ
SOUR MIX

THIS ONE DEFINITELY CALLS FOR A MARTINI GLASS.

YOU PRETTY MUCH HAVE EVERYTHING YOU NEED:

■ JUST MAKE SURE YOU HAVE A LEMON

OH, AND YOU'LL ALSO NEED TO HAVE SOME MINT HANDY

THE 1ST SODA IN THE U.S. WAS VERNOR'S GINGER ALE,
CREATED IN DETROIT, MI, IN 1866 BY JAMES VERNOR.

INGREDIENTS	INSTRUCTIONS
■ 3 MINT LEAVES	GET SHAKER ☐
■ 3 LEMON WEDGES	ADD LEMON & MINT ☐
■ 2 OZ BOURBON	MUDDLE & FILL W/ ICE ☐
■ 1 OZ GINGER ALE	ADD OTHER INGREDIENTS ☐
■ MINT LEAF (GARNISH)	SHAKE UNTIL CHILLED ☐
■ LEMON (GARNISH)	FILL SERVING GLASS W/ ICE ☐
	STRAIN INTO GLASS ☐
	GARNISH W/ LEMON WEDGE ☐
	ADD MINT LEAF ☐

WHAT DO YOU THINK?

. . . .

DRINK THIS AGAIN?   YES ☐   NO ☐   IF DESPERATE ☐

BONUS TRIVIA

REDHEADS TYPICALLY HAVE LESS HAIR THAN OTHER PEOPLE. ON AVERAGE, THEY ONLY HAVE ABOUT 90,000 STRANDS OF HAIR ON THEIR HEAD, WHILE BRUNETTES NORMALLY HAVE UPWARDS OF 140,000.

EACH STRAND IS CONSIDERABLY THICKER, THOUGH, SO THEIR HAIR LOOKS JUST AS FULL.

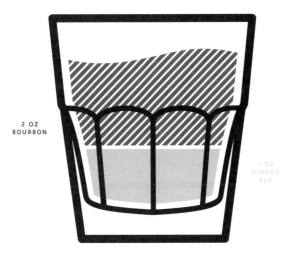

2 OZ
BOURBON

1 OZ
GINGER
ALE

WE'D RECOMMEND A LOWBALL GLASS FOR THIS ONE.

YOU PRETTY MUCH HAVE EVERYTHING YOU NEED:

JUST MAKE SURE YOU HAVE A LIME

AND MAYBE CHECK THE FRESHNESS OF THAT JUICE

DON'T JUST USE ANY DARK RUM, UNLESS YOU WANT TO GET SUED. GOSLINGS TRADEMARKED THE RECIPE.*

INGREDIENTS

- 2 OZ GOSLINGS BLACK SEAL RUM
- .5 OZ LIME JUICE
- GINGER BEER
- LIME (GARNISH)

INSTRUCTIONS

- GET GLASS ☐
- FILL WITH ICE ☐
- ADD FIRST 2 INGREDIENTS ☐
- TOP WITH GINGER BEER ☐
- GARNISH W/ LIME WEDGE ☐

WHAT DO YOU THINK?

. . . .

. . . .

. . . .

*AND WE HEAR THEY REALLY MEAN BUSINESS.

DRINK THIS AGAIN?   YES ☐   NO ☐   IF DESPERATE ☐

BONUS TRIVIA

REPORTEDLY, IT'S A PERSONAL FAVORITE OF MINDY KALING.
BE CAREFUL WITH THE RUM SELECTION, MINDY.

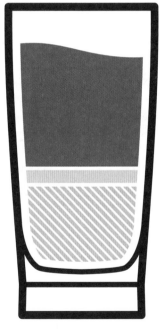

GINGER
BEER

5 OZ
LIME JUICE

2 OZ
GOSLINGS
BLACK
SEAL RUM*

LEGALLY, YOU SHOULD USE A HIGHBALL GLASS.

FIRST THINGS FIRST, GO BUY SOME:

CACHAÇA (PRONOUNCED KAH-SHAA-SAH)

OH, AND YOU'LL ALSO NEED SOME LIMES (AND SUGAR)

IN 2013, JOHN TRAVOLTA STARRED IN AN...INTERESTING BRAZILIAN AD FOR YPICOCA BRAND CACHAÇA. LOOK IT UP.

INGREDIENTS	INSTRUCTIONS
2 OZ CACHAÇA	GET SERVING GLASS ☐
2 TSP SUGAR	ADD LIME WEDGES & SUGAR ☐
3 LIME WEDGES	MUDDLE UNTIL MIXED ☐
LIME (GARNISH)	FILL W/ ICE & ADD CACHAÇA ☐
	STIR TO COMBINE ☐
	GARNISH W/ LIME SLICE ☐

WHAT DO YOU THINK?

. . . .

. . . .

. . . .

DRINK THIS AGAIN? YES ☐ NO ☐ IF DESPERATE ☐

BONUS TRIVIA

BRAZILIAN LAW (SPECIFICALLY, LEI DE CAIPIRINHA OR CAIPIRINHA LAW) STATES THAT A CAIPIRINHA CAN ONLY BE CALLED AS SUCH IF IT'S MADE WITH CACHAÇA AND MIXED ONLY WITH LIME AND SUGAR. NO OTHER FRUITS OR ADDITIONS ARE ALLOWED...

OR ELSE.

2 OZ
CACHAÇA

2 TSP
SUGAR

WE'D RECOMMEND A LOWBALL GLASS FOR THIS ONE.

YOU PRETTY MUCH HAVE EVERYTHING YOU NEED:

JUST CHECK THE FRESHNESS OF THAT LIME JUICE

AND MAYBE SEE IF YOU'RE GETTING LOW ON ANYTHING

THE HUMAN FEMUR IS STRONGER THAN CONCRETE.
THAT PINKY TOE? WELL, IT MIGHT AS WELL BE GLASS.

INGREDIENTS

- 2 OZ RYE WHISKEY
- 1 TSP LIME JUICE
- 1 TSP SIMPLE SYRUP
- 3 DASH TABASCO SAUCE

INSTRUCTIONS

- GET MIXING GLASS ☐
- FILL WITH ICE ☐
- ADD ALL INGREDIENTS ☐
- STIR UNTIL CHILLED ☐
- STRAIN INTO GLASS ☐

WHAT DO YOU THINK?

. . . .

. . . .

. . . .

. . . .

DRINK THIS AGAIN?   YES ☐   NO ☐   IF DESPERATE ☐

BONUS TRIVIA

ORIGINALLY CREATED BY DAVID WONDRICH FOR THE (NOW CLOSED) 'CHICKENBONE CAFÉ' IN BROOKLYN, NY.

2 OZ
RYE
WHISKEY

1 TSP
LIME JUICE

1 TSP
SIMPLE SUGAR

3 DASH
TABASCO
SAUCE

IF IT WERE US, WE'D USE A MARTINI GLASS.

FIRST THINGS FIRST, GO BUY SOME:

ORANGE LIQUEUR

OH, AND YOU'LL ALSO NEED A BRANDIED CHERRY

THE OFFICIAL COCKTAIL OF THE PREAKNESS (A HORSE RACE / EXCUSE TO GET DRESSED UP AND DRINK).

INGREDIENTS	INSTRUCTIONS
2 OZ PINEAPPLE JUICE	GET SERVING GLASS ☐
.5 OZ VODKA	FILL WITH ICE ☐
.5 OZ WHITE RUM	ADD FIRST 4 INGREDIENTS ☐
.25 OZ ORANGE LIQUEUR	STIR UNTIL CHILLED ☐
3 OZ ORANGE JUICE	ADD ORANGE JUICE ☐
BRANDIED CHERRY (GARNISH)	GARNISH W/ CHERRY ☐

WHAT DO YOU THINK?

. . . .

. . . .

. . . .

. . . .

DRINK THIS AGAIN?   YES ☐   NO ☐   IF DESPERATE ☐

BONUS TRIVIA

IN THE LANGUAGE OF FLOWERS (YEP, THAT'S A THING),
BLACK-EYED SUSANS REPRESENT ENCOURAGEMENT.

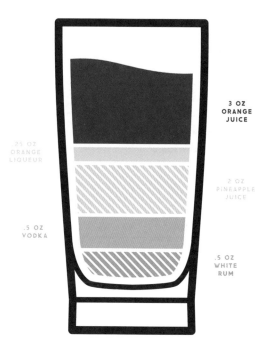

3 OZ
ORANGE
JUICE

.25 OZ
ORANGE
LIQUEUR

2 OZ
PINEAPPLE
JUICE

.5 OZ
VODKA

.5 OZ
WHITE
RUM

YOU SHOULD PROBABLY USE A HIGHBALL GLASS.

YOU PRETTY MUCH HAVE EVERYTHING YOU NEED:

JUST MAKE SURE YOU HAVE A BRANDIED CHERRY

AND MAYBE CHECK THE FRESHNESS OF THAT CRANBERRY JUICE

THE FIRST MODERN FLUSHABLE TOILET WAS INVENTED
(AND INSTALLED) FOR QUEEN ELIZABETH I IN 1959.

INGREDIENTS

1.5 OZ TENNESSEE WHISKEY
2 OZ PEACH LIQUEUR
.5 OZ RASPBERRY LIQUEUR
2 OZ CRANBERRY JUICE
BRANDIED CHERRY (GARNISH)

INSTRUCTIONS

GET SHAKER ☐
FILL WITH ICE ☐
ADD ALL INGREDIENTS ☐
SHAKE UNTIL CHILLED ☐
GET GLASS & ADD ICE ☐
STRAIN INTO GLASS ☐
GARNISH W/ CHERRY ☐

WHAT DO YOU THINK?

. . . .

. . . .

. . . .

. . . .

DRINK THIS AGAIN?   YES ☐   NO ☐   IF DESPERATE ☐

BONUS TRIVIA

IN A STANDARD POKER GAME, THE ODDS OF BEING DEALT A ROYAL FLUSH WITH YOUR FIRST FIVE CARDS ARE JUST 1 IN 649,740. BUT HEY, THOSE ODDS ARE STILL BETTER THAN:

WINNING AN OLYMPIC GOLD MEDAL: 1 IN 662,000
BEING ATTACKED BY A SHARK: 1 IN 11,500,000
OR DYING VIA VENDING MACHINE: 1 IN 112,000,000

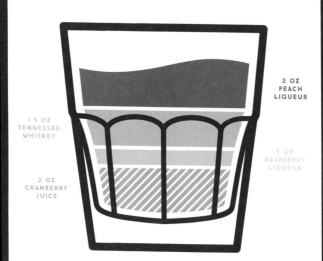

2 OZ
PEACH
LIQUEUR

1.5 OZ
TENNESSEE
WHISKEY

.5 OZ
RASPBERRY
LIQUEUR

2 OZ
CRANBERRY
JUICE

WE'D RECOMMEND A LOWBALL GLASS FOR THIS ONE.

YOU PRETTY MUCH HAVE EVERYTHING YOU NEED:

█ JUST MAKE SURE YOU HAVE A LEMON

CHECK YOUR BAR FOR ANYTHING YOU'RE GETTING LOW ON, THOUGH

JUST IN CASE YOU DON'T KNOW FRENCH (LIKE US),
'TREMBLEMENT DE TERRE' MEANS 'EARTHQUAKE.'

INGREDIENTS   **INSTRUCTIONS**

█ 2.5 OZ ABSINTHE   CHILL SERVING GLASS ☐

█ .25 OZ COGNAC   GET SHAKER & ADD ICE ☐

█ LEMON (GARNISH)   ADD ALL INGREDIENTS ☐

SHAKE UNTIL CHILLED ☐

STRAIN INTO SERVING GLASS ☐

GARNISH W/ LEMON TWIST ☐

WHAT DO YOU THINK?

. . . .

. . . .

. . . .

DRINK THIS AGAIN?   YES ☐   NO ☐   IF DESPERATE ☐

HENRI DE TOULOUSE-LAUTREC SUPPOSEDLY SERVED THESE AT HIS
PARTIES. IF YOU DIDN'T GO TO ART SCHOOL, HE WAS A PAINTER.

2.5 OZ
ABSINTHE

.25 OZ
COGNAC

THIS ONE DEFINITELY CALLS FOR A MARTINI GLASS.

FIRST THINGS FIRST, GO BUY SOME:

ROSE WATER

AND MAYBE CHECK THE FRESHNESS OF THAT GRAPEFRUIT JUICE

THE FIRST THING THAT BUZZ ALDRIN & NEIL ARMSTRONG
DRANK AFTER RETURNING TO EARTH IN 1969. PROBABLY.

INGREDIENTS	INSTRUCTIONS
1 OZ ORANGE LIQUEUR	GET SHAKER & ADD ICE ☐
1 OZ GRAPEFRUIT JUICE	ADD FIRST 3 INGREDIENTS ☐
3 DASH ROSE WATER	SHAKE UNTIL CHILLED ☐
CHAMPAGNE	STRAIN INTO SERVING GLASS ☐
	TOP W/ CHAMPAGNE ☐

WHAT DO YOU THINK?

. . . .

. . . .

. . . .

. . . .

DRINK THIS AGAIN?   YES ☐   NO ☐   IF DESPERATE ☐

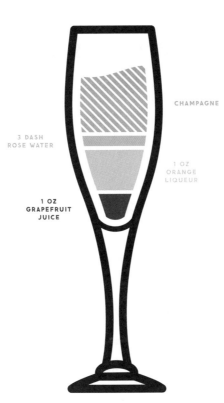

CHAMPAGNE

3 DASH
ROSE WATER

1 OZ
ORANGE
LIQUEUR

1 OZ
GRAPEFRUIT
JUICE

FINALLY, A USE FOR THOSE CHAMPAGNE FLUTES.

YOU PRETTY MUCH HAVE EVERYTHING YOU NEED:

JUST MAKE SURE THAT YOUR JUICE IS STILL FRESH

OH, AND YOU'LL ALSO NEED SOME PINEAPPLE

CREATED BY HARRY YEE IN 1957, TWO YEARS BEFORE
HAWAII WOULD OFFICIALLY BECOME A U.S. STATE.

INGREDIENTS

.75 OZ WHITE RUM
.75 OZ VODKA
.5 OZ CURAÇAO
3 OZ PINEAPPLE JUICE
1 OZ SOUR MIX
PINEAPPLE (GARNISH)

INSTRUCTIONS

GET SHAKER & ADD ICE ☐
ADD ALL INGREDIENTS ☐
SHAKE UNTIL CHILLED ☐
GET SERVING GLASS ☐
FILL WITH ICE ☐
STRAIN INTO GLASS ☐
GARNISH W/ PINEAPPLE WEDGE ☐

WHAT DO YOU THINK?

. . . .

. . . .

DRINK THIS AGAIN?   YES ☐   NO ☐   IF DESPERATE ☐

DESPITE POPULAR BELIEF, THIS DRINK WASN'T NAMED AFTER THE
1961 ELVIS MOVIE. IN FACT, IT WAS LIKELY THE OPPOSITE.

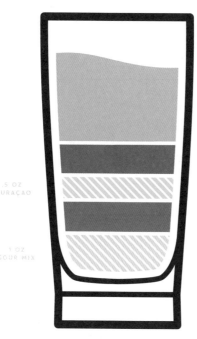

3 OZ
PINEAPPLE
JUICE

.75 OZ
WHITE RUM

.5 OZ
CURAÇAO

.75 OZ
VODKA

1 OZ
SOUR MIX

YOU SHOULD PROBABLY USE A HIGHBALL GLASS.

FIRST THINGS FIRST, GO BUY SOME:

■ AGAVE NECTAR

OH, AND YOU'LL ALSO NEED A LIME OR TWO

A GREAT TEQUILA-BASED VARIANT OF THE TOM COLLINS (AND AN EVEN BETTER PUN).

INGREDIENTS

- 1.5 OZ BLANCO TEQUILA
- 1 OZ LEMON JUICE
- .5 OZ AGAVE NECTAR
- 2 OZ CLUB SODA
- LIME (GARNISH)

INSTRUCTIONS

GET SERVING GLASS ☐
FILL WITH ICE ☐
ADD FIRST 3 INGREDIENTS ☐
STIR UNTIL CHILLED ☐
TOP WITH CLUB SODA ☐
GARNISH W/ LIME SLICE ☐

WHAT DO YOU THINK?

. . . .

. . . .

. . . .

DRINK THIS AGAIN?   YES ☐   NO ☐   IF DESPERATE ☐

BONUS TRIVIA

AGAVE PLANTS ARE PRIMARILY POLLINATED BY THE MEXICAN
LONG-NOSED BAT. IT'S ESSENTIALLY A FURRY HUMMINGBIRD.

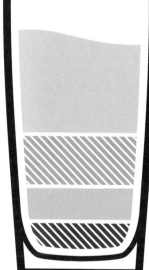

2 OZ
CLUB SODA

1.5 OZ
BLANCO
TEQUILA

1 OZ
LEMON JUICE

.5 OZ
AGAVE NECTAR

YOU SHOULD PROBABLY USE A HIGHBALL GLASS.

YOU PRETTY MUCH HAVE EVERYTHING YOU NEED:

WELL, TO MAKE THE DRINK WITH ANYWAY

CHECK YOUR BAR FOR ANYTHING YOU'RE GETTING LOW ON, THOUGH

> IN CASE YOU'VE BEEN WONDERING HOW TO SAY
> PEYCHAUD'S, IT'S PRONOUNCED PAY-SHOWS.

INGREDIENTS

- 2 OZ BOURBON
- 2 DASH PEYCHAUD'S BITTERS
- 1 DASH GRENADINE

INSTRUCTIONS

- GET SERVING GLASS ☐
- FILL WITH ICE ☐
- ADD ALL INGREDIENTS ☐
- STIR TO COMBINE ☐

WHAT DO YOU THINK?

. . . .

. . . .

. . . .

. . . .

. . . .

. . . .

DRINK THIS AGAIN?   YES ☐   NO ☐   IF DESPERATE ☐

BONUS TRIVIA

SORRY, DESPITE WHAT THE INTERNET CLAIMS, THERE IS NO
SUCH THING AS A NATURALLY OCCURRING BLACK ROSE. THE
'FAMED' TURKISH HALFETI ROSE SEEMS TO BE AS CLOSE
AS IT GETS, BUT AT BEST, IT'S SIMPLY A REALLY DARK RED.

GO AHEAD, GOOGLE IT. WASTE AN HOUR OF YOUR LIFE
DOWN THAT RABBIT HOLE LIKE WE JUST DID.

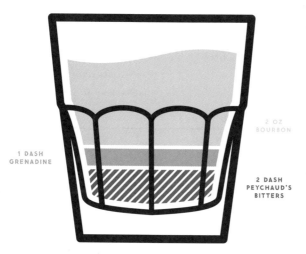

1 DASH
GRENADINE

2 OZ
BOURBON

2 DASH
PEYCHAUD'S
BITTERS

WE'D RECOMMEND A LOWBALL GLASS FOR THIS ONE.

YOU PRETTY MUCH HAVE EVERYTHING YOU NEED:

JUST CHECK THE FRESHNESS OF THAT CRANBERRY JUICE

OH, AND YOU'LL ALSO NEED A LIME

ORIGINALLY THIS DRINK WAS CALLED THE TEENY
WEENY WOO WOO. ODDLY, IT WAS LATER SHORTENED.

INGREDIENTS	INSTRUCTIONS
1 OZ VODKA	GET SHAKER & FILL W/ ICE ☐
2 OZ CRANBERRY JUICE	ADD ALL INGREDIENTS ☐
1 OZ PEACH LIQUEUR	SHAKE UNTIL CHILLED ☐
LIME (GARNISH)	GET SERVING GLASS & ADD ICE ☐
	STRAIN INTO GLASS ☐
	GARNISH W/ LIME SLICE ☐

WHAT DO YOU THINK?

. . . .

. . . .

. . . .

DRINK THIS AGAIN?   YES ☐   NO ☐   IF DESPERATE ☐

BONUS TRIVIA

CREATED IN THE EARLY 1980s, WAY BEFORE WOO GIRLS STARTED
RUINING EVERY CONCERT THAT YOU WENT TO.

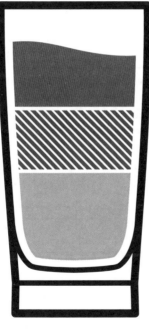

1 OZ
VODKA

1 OZ
PEACH
LIQUEUR

2 OZ
CRANBERRY
JUICE

YOU SHOULD PROBABLY USE A HIGHBALL GLASS.

FIRST THINGS FIRST, GO BUY SOME:

CRÈME DE CASSIS

OH, AND YOU'LL ALSO NEED AN ORANGE

SUPPOSEDLY THIS COCKTAIL WAS INSPIRED BY A SCENE
IN THE 1953 FILM 'FROM HERE TO ETERNITY.'

INGREDIENTS   **INSTRUCTIONS**

1.5 OZ VODKA   GET SHAKER & ADD ICE ☐

.5 OZ PEACH LIQUEUR   ADD ALL INGREDIENTS ☐

1.5 OZ ORANGE JUICE   SHAKE UNTIL CHILLED ☐

1.5 OZ CRANBERRY JUICE   GET SERVING GLASS ☐

.5 OZ CRÈME DE CASSIS   FILL WITH ICE ☐

ORANGE (GARNISH)   STRAIN INTO GLASS ☐

                           GARNISH W/ ORANGE SLICE ☐

WHAT DO YOU THINK?

. . . .

. . . .

DRINK THIS AGAIN?   YES ☐   NO ☐   IF DESPERATE ☐

117 MAKE A SEX ON THE BEACH

BONUS TRIVIA

DOESN'T THE TITLE ON THIS PAGE SOUND LIKE SOMETHING AN R-RATED SUPER MARIO WOULD SAY? HELP, WE'RE SO TIRED.

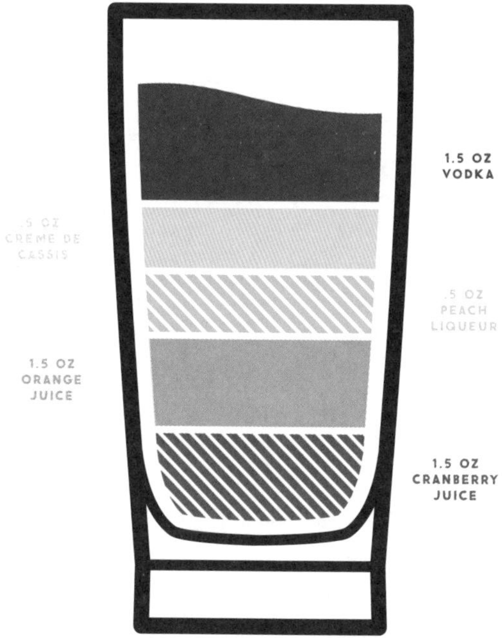

1.5 OZ
VODKA
.5 OZ
CREME DE
CASSIS
.5 OZ
PEACH
LIQUEUR
1.5 OZ
ORANGE
JUICE
1.5 OZ
CRANBERRY
JUICE

YOU SHOULD PROBABLY USE A HIGHBALL GLASS.

FIRST THINGS FIRST, GO BUY SOME:

PASSION FRUIT JUICE

OH, AND YOU'LL ALSO NEED BRANDIED CHERRIES (AND AN ORANGE)

CREATED IN THE 1940s BY TAVERN OWNER PAT O'BRIEN.
HE WAS JUST TRYING TO GET RID OF OLD RUM.

INGREDIENTS	INSTRUCTIONS
2 OZ WHITE RUM	GET SHAKER & ADD ICE ☐
2 OZ DARK RUM	ADD ALL INGREDIENTS ☐
1 OZ ORANGE JUICE	SHAKE UNTIL CHILLED ☐
2 OZ PASSION FRUIT JUICE	GET SERVING GLASS ☐
.5 OZ LIME JUICE	FILL WITH ICE ☐
1 TBSP GRENADINE	STRAIN INTO GLASS ☐
1 TBSP SIMPLE SYRUP	GARNISH W/ ORANGE SLICE ☐
ORANGE (GARNISH)	ADD CHERRY ☐
BRANDIED CHERRY (GARNISH)	

WHAT DO YOU THINK?

DRINK THIS AGAIN?   YES ☐   NO ☐   IF DESPERATE ☐

BONUS TRIVIA

OVER 40 PERCENT OF THE HURRICANES THAT HAVE REACHED
THE UNITED STATES HAVE ALSO HIT FLORIDA.

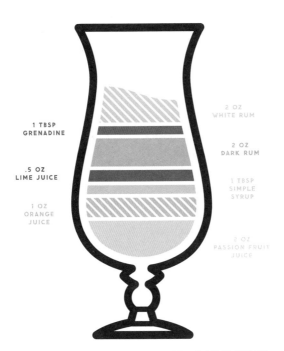

1 TBSP
GRENADINE

.5 OZ
LIME JUICE

1 OZ
ORANGE
JUICE

2 OZ
WHITE RUM

2 OZ
DARK RUM

1 TBSP
SIMPLE
SYRUP

2 OZ
PASSION FRUIT
JUICE

USE THE HURRICANE GLASS YOU STOLE ON VACATION.

YOU PRETTY MUCH HAVE EVERYTHING YOU NEED:

☐ JUST MAKE SURE YOU HAVE AN ORANGE

CHECK YOUR BAR FOR ANYTHING YOU'RE GETTING LOW ON, THOUGH

THE ANGOSTURA BITTERS ARE SAID TO REPRESENT
THE FEELING OF PAYING THE GOVERNMENT.

INGREDIENTS

- 1.5 OZ DRY GIN
- .75 OZ DRY VERMOUTH
- .75 OZ SWEET VERMOUTH
- .5 OZ ORANGE JUICE
- 2 DASH ANGOSTURA BITTERS
- ORANGE (GARNISH)

INSTRUCTIONS

GET MIXING GLASS ☐
FILL WITH ICE ☐
ADD ALL INGREDIENTS ☐
SHAKE UNTIL CHILLED ☐
GET SERVING GLASS ☐
STRAIN INTO GLASS ☐
GARNISH W/ ORANGE TWIST ☐

WHAT DO YOU THINK?

. . . .

. . . .

DRINK THIS AGAIN?   YES ☐   NO ☐   IF DESPERATE ☐

IN 1991, AN EXOTIC DANCER NAMED CYNTHIA HESS (AKA CHESTY LOVE) WAS PERMITTED TO WRITE OFF THE COST OF HER SIZE 56N BREAST IMPLANTS AS ESSENTIAL TO HER PERFORMANCE.

1.5 OZ DRY GIN

.75 OZ SWEET VERMOUTH

.75 OZ DRY VERMOUTH

.5 OZ ORANGE JUICE

2 DASH ANGOSTURA BITTERS

USE A COUPE GLASS. TRUST US, IT'S WORTH IT.

FIRST THINGS FIRST, GO BUY SOME:

HONEY SYRUP (YOU CAN ALSO MAKE IT, BTW)

CHECK YOUR BAR FOR ANYTHING YOU'RE GETTING LOW ON, THOUGH

HONEY SYRUP IS JUST HONEY THAT'S BEEN DISSOLVED INTO AN EQUAL AMOUNT OF WATER (OVER HEAT).

INGREDIENTS	INSTRUCTIONS
1.5 OZ RYE WHISKEY	CHILL SERVING GLASS ☐
.75 OZ GRAPEFRUIT JUICE	GET SHAKER & ADD ICE ☐
.75 OZ HONEY SYRUP	ADD ALL INGREDIENTS ☐
	SHAKE UNTIL CHILLED ☐
	STRAIN INTO GLASS ☐

WHAT DO YOU THINK?

. . . .

. . . .

. . . .

. . . .

DRINK THIS AGAIN?　　YES ☐　　NO ☐　　IF DESPERATE ☐

THIS WAS THE SIGNATURE DRINK OF THE 1919 BROADWAY PLAY
OF THE SAME NAME. THE SHOW WAS LATER ADAPTED INTO TWO
FEATURE FILMS THAT WE HAVE ALSO NEVER HEARD OF.

1.5 OZ
RYE
WHISKEY

.75 OZ
HONEY
SYRUP

.75 OZ
GRAPEFRUIT
JUICE

YOU SHOULD PROBABLY USE A COUPE GLASS.

YOU PRETTY MUCH HAVE EVERYTHING YOU NEED:

■ JUST MAKE SURE YOU HAVE A LEMON

OH, AND YOU'LL ALSO NEED SOME MINT

A SMASH IS A TYPE OF JULEP, BUT A JULEP ISN'T ALWAYS A SMASH. IT'S KIND OF COMPLICATED.

INGREDIENTS

■ 3 LEMON WEDGES
■ .75 OZ SIMPLE SYRUP
■ 2 OZ BOURBON
■ 4 MINT LEAVES
■ MINT SPRIG (GARNISH)

INSTRUCTIONS

GET SHAKER ☐
ADD LEMON WEDGES ☐
MUDDLE & FILL W/ ICE ☐
ADD ALL INGREDIENTS ☐
SHAKE UNTIL CHILLED ☐
GET GLASS & ADD ICE ☐
STRAIN INTO GLASS ☐
GARNISH W/ MINT SPRIG ☐

WHAT DO YOU THINK?

. . . .

. . . .

DRINK THIS AGAIN?   YES ☐   NO ☐   IF DESPERATE ☐

BONUS TRIVIA

THE KEY TO MAKING A GOOD SMASH IS A GOOD MUDDLER. THE GOAL IS TO NOT ONLY RELEASE THE JUICES IN THE LEMON WEDGES, BUT THE OILS IN THE PEEL AS WELL. THIS CREATES A RICHER TASTE WHEN COMBINED WITH THE OTHER INGREDIENTS.

IN OTHER WORDS, MUDDLE THE CRAP OUT OF THEM.

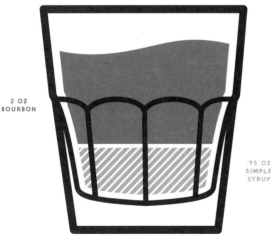

2 OZ
BOURBON

.75 OZ
SIMPLE
SYRUP

WE'D RECOMMEND A LOWBALL GLASS FOR THIS ONE.

YOU PRETTY MUCH HAVE EVERYTHING YOU NEED:

☐ JUST MAKE SURE YOU HAVE A LIME

CHECK YOUR BAR FOR ANYTHING YOU'RE GETTING LOW ON, THOUGH

> WHILE SEEMINGLY IMPOSSIBLE, THIS DRINK IS THE
> BOOZIER COUSIN OF THE LONG ISLAND ICED TEA.

INGREDIENTS

☐ 1 OZ BLANCO TEQUILA
☐ 1 OZ VODKA
☐ 1 OZ WHITE RUM
☐ 1 OZ DRY GIN
☐ 1 OZ ORANGE LIQUEUR
☐ 1 OZ RASPBERRY LIQUEUR
☐ 2 OZ SOUR MIX
☐ LIME (GARNISH)

INSTRUCTIONS

GET SHAKER & ADD ICE ☐
ADD ALL INGREDIENTS ☐
SHAKE UNTIL CHILLED ☐
GET SERVING GLASS ☐
FILL WITH ICE ☐
STRAIN INTO GLASS ☐
GARNISH W/ LIME SLICE ☐

WHAT DO YOU THINK?

. . . .

. . . .

DRINK THIS AGAIN?   YES ☐   NO ☐   IF DESPERATE ☐

BONUS TRIVIA

IN 1991, THE GRATEFUL DEAD HELPED PAY TO GET LITHUANIA'S
BASKETBALL TEAM TO THE OLYMPICS. THEY WON BRONZE.

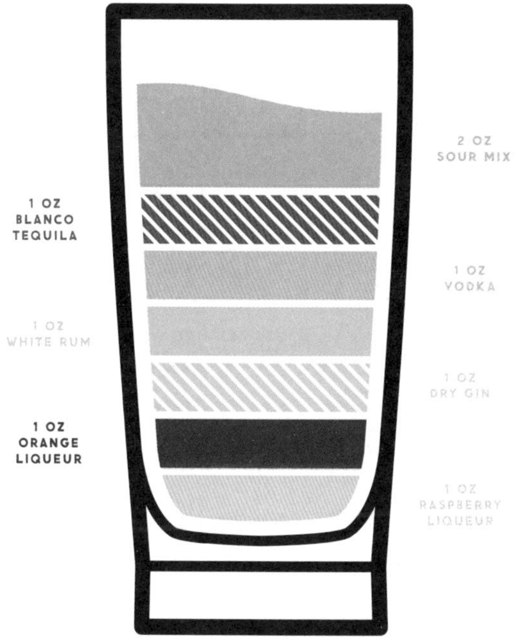

2 OZ
SOUR MIX

1 OZ
BLANCO
TEQUILA

1 OZ
VODKA

1 OZ
WHITE RUM

1 OZ
DRY GIN

1 OZ
ORANGE
LIQUEUR

1 OZ
RASPBERRY
LIQUEUR

YOU SHOULD PROBABLY USE A HIGHBALL GLASS.

FIRST THINGS FIRST, GO BUY SOME:

■ SAKÉ (LOOK FOR THE WORD JUNMAI, IT'S THE PUREST)

OH, AND YOU'LL ALSO NEED SUGAR, MINT, AND A LIME

ALTHOUGH COMMONLY REFERRED TO AS RICE WINE,
SAKÉ PRODUCTION IS CLOSER TO THAT OF BEER.

INGREDIENTS	INSTRUCTIONS
1 TSP SUGAR	GET SHAKER ☐
6 MINT LEAVES	ADD FIRST 3 INGREDIENTS ☐
4 LIME WEDGES	MUDDLE UNTIL MIXED ☐
5 OZ SAKÉ	FILL WITH ICE & ADD SAKÉ ☐
1 OZ CLUB SODA	SHAKE UNTIL CHILLED ☐
	GET SERVING GLASS & ADD ICE ☐
	STRAIN INTO GLASS ☐
	TOP WITH CLUB SODA ☐

WHAT DO YOU THINK?

. . . .

. . . .

DRINK THIS AGAIN?   YES ☐   NO ☐   IF DESPERATE ☐

BONUS TRIVIA

AT ONE TIME, SAKÉ WAS MADE BY CHEWING & SPITTING MASHED RICE INTO COMMUNAL TUBS. THE SALIVA AIDED FERMENTATION.

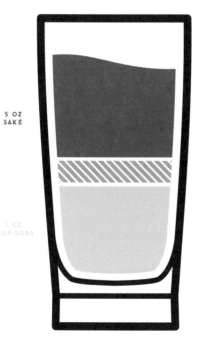

5 OZ
SAKÉ

1 TSP
SUGAR

1 OZ
CLUB SODA

YOU SHOULD PROBABLY USE A HIGHBALL GLASS.

YOU PRETTY MUCH HAVE EVERYTHING YOU NEED:

JUST CHECK THE FRESHNESS OF THAT LIME JUICE

CHECK YOUR BAR FOR ANYTHING YOU'RE GETTING LOW ON, THOUGH

THIS DRINK WAS ORIGINALLY CALLED AN ORIENTAL.
TIMES HAVE CHANGED, AND SO HAS THE NAME.

INGREDIENTS

- 1.5 OZ RYE WHISKEY
- .75 OZ SWEET VERMOUTH
- .75 OZ TRIPLE SEC
- .5 OZ LIME JUICE

INSTRUCTIONS

- GET SHAKER & ADD ICE ☐
- ADD ALL INGREDIENTS ☐
- SHAKE UNTIL CHILLED ☐
- STRAIN INTO SERVING GLASS ☐

WHAT DO YOU THINK?

. . . .

. . . .

. . . .

. . . .

. . . .

. . . .

DRINK THIS AGAIN?   YES ☐   NO ☐   IF DESPERATE ☐

SUPPOSEDLY, IN 1924, A MAN THAT NEARLY DIED OF FEVER IN THE
PHILIPPINES GAVE THE RECIPE TO THE DOCTOR THAT SAVED HIM.

1.5 OZ
RYE WHISKEY

.75 OZ SWEET
VERMOUTH

.75 OZ
TRIPLE SEC

.5 OZ
LIME JUICE

THIS ONE DEFINITELY CALLS FOR A MARTINI GLASS.

YOU PRETTY MUCH HAVE EVERYTHING YOU NEED:

■ JUST MAKE SURE YOU HAVE AN EXTRA LIME

AND MAYBE CHECK THE FRESHNESS OF THAT CRANBERRY JUICE

ADJUSTED FOR INFLATION, 'GONE WITH THE WIND' IS THE HIGHEST GROSSING FILM OF ALL TIME ($3.4 BIL).

INGREDIENTS

■ 3 OZ TENNESSEE WHISKEY
■ 1.5 OZ LIME JUICE
■ 3 OZ CRANBERRY JUICE
■ LIME (GARNISH)

INSTRUCTIONS

GET SERVING GLASS ☐
FILL WITH ICE ☐
ADD FIRST 2 INGREDIENTS ☐
TOP WITH CRANBERRY JUICE ☐
STIR UNTIL CHILLED ☐
GARNISH W/ LIME WEDGE ☐

WHAT DO YOU THINK?

. . . .

. . . .

. . . .

DRINK THIS AGAIN?   YES ☐   NO ☐   IF DESPERATE ☐

BONUS TRIVIA

NAMED AFTER THE LEADING LADY OF THE FILM, THIS DRINK
WAS CREATED IN 1939 TO PROMOTE ITS RELEASE.

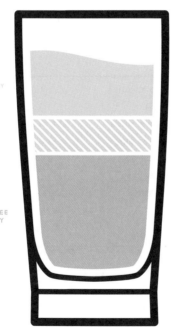

3 OZ
CRANBERRY
JUICE

1.5 OZ
LIME JUICE

3 OZ
TENNESSEE
WHISKEY

YOU SHOULD PROBABLY USE A HIGHBALL GLASS.

FIRST THINGS FIRST, GO BUY SOME:

REPOSADO TEQUILA

OH, AND YOU'LL ALSO NEED SOME PINEAPPLE

'REPOSADO' TRANSLATES TO 'RESTED,' & THAT'S EXACTLY
WHAT IT IS. UNLIKE BLANCO, IT'S AGED FOR 2-12 MONTHS.

INGREDIENTS

- 1 OZ REPOSADO TEQUILA
- 1 OZ WHITE RUM
- .75 OZ PINEAPPLE JUICE
- .5 OZ GRAPEFRUIT JUICE
- .5 OZ LIME JUICE
- .25 OZ AGAVE NECTAR
- PINEAPPLE (GARNISH)

INSTRUCTIONS

- GET SHAKER ☐
- FILL WITH ICE ☐
- ADD ALL INGREDIENTS ☐
- SHAKE UNTIL CHILLED ☐
- GET SERVING GLASS ☐
- FILL WITH ICE ☐
- STRAIN INTO GLASS ☐
- GARNISH W/ PINEAPPLE WEDGE ☐

WHAT DO YOU THINK?

. . . .

. . . .

DRINK THIS AGAIN?   YES ☐   NO ☐   IF DESPERATE ☐

BONUS TRIVIA

DESPITE THE NAME OF HIS 1963 FILM 'FUN IN ACAPULCO,' ELVIS
PRESLEY NEVER FILMED THERE.

MORE SPECIFICALLY, HE WAS BARRED FROM EVEN ENTERING
INTO MEXICO AFTER BEING DECLARED A 'PERSONA NON GRATA'
BY THE MEXICAN GOVERNMENT. THEY CITED UNRULY BEHAVIOR
BY HIS FANS, BUT THE REASON IS RUMORED TO BE HIS REFUSAL
TO GIVE A PRIVATE CONCERT FOR A POLITICIAN'S DAUGHTER.

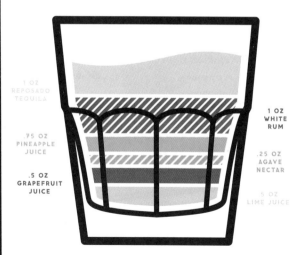

1 OZ
REPOSADO
TEQUILA

.75 OZ
PINEAPPLE
JUICE

.5 OZ
GRAPEFRUIT
JUICE

1 OZ
WHITE
RUM

.25 OZ
AGAVE
NECTAR

.5 OZ
LIME JUICE

WE'D RECOMMEND A LOWBALL GLASS FOR THIS ONE.

YOU PRETTY MUCH HAVE EVERYTHING YOU NEED:

■ JUST MAKE SURE THAT LIME JUICE IS STILL GOOD

CHECK YOUR BAR FOR ANYTHING YOU'RE GETTING LOW ON, THOUGH

VICTOR BERGERON REPORTEDLY CREATED IT TO MOCK
HIS TIKI BAR COMPETITOR, DON THE BEACHCOMBER.

INGREDIENTS

■ 2 OZ WHITE RUM
■ .75 OZ TRIPLE SEC
■ .75 OZ LIME JUICE
■ .25 OZ MARASCHINO LIQUEUR
■ .25 OZ SIMPLE SYRUP

INSTRUCTIONS

CHILL SERVING GLASS ☐
GET SHAKER & ADD ICE ☐
ADD ALL INGREDIENTS ☐
SHAKE UNTIL MIXED ☐
STRAIN INTO GLASS ☐

WHAT DO YOU THINK?

. . . .

. . . .

. . . .

. . . .

DRINK THIS AGAIN?   YES ☐   NO ☐   IF DESPERATE ☐

BONUS TRIVIA

IN 2012, 8-YEAR-OLD CHARLIE NEYSMITH PICKED UP WHAT HE
THOUGHT WAS A LARGE WAXY ROCK ON A BEACH IN GREAT
BRITAIN. IT WAS ACTUALLY AMBERGRIS (AKA WHALE VOMIT)
VALUED AT OVER $63,000. SERIOUSLY.

2 OZ
WHITE RUM

.25 OZ
SIMPLE SYRUP

.75 OZ
TRIPLE SEC

.25 OZ
LIME JUICE

.25 OZ
MARASCHINO
LIQUEUR

USE A COUPE GLASS. TRUST US, IT'S WORTH IT.

YOU PRETTY MUCH HAVE EVERYTHING YOU NEED:

JUST MAKE SURE YOU HAVE FRESH CREAM (AND A COKE)

OH, AND YOU'LL ALSO NEED A BRANDIED CHERRY

PRO-TIP: TO REDUCE THE CHANCE OF CURDLED CREAM, POUR SLOWLY WHILE STIRRING THE TOP OF THE DRINK.

INGREDIENTS

1 OZ VODKA
1 OZ COFFEE LIQUEUR
5 OZ COCA-COLA
1 OZ CREAM
BRANDIED CHERRY (GARNISH)

INSTRUCTIONS

GET SERVING GLASS ☐
FILL WITH ICE ☐
ADD FIRST 2 INGREDIENTS ☐
ADD COCA-COLA ☐
STIR GENTLY ☐
SLOWLY TOP W/ CREAM ☐
GARNISH W/ CHERRY ☐

WHAT DO YOU THINK?

. . . .

. . . .

DRINK THIS AGAIN?   YES ☐   NO ☐   IF DESPERATE ☐

MAKE A PARALYZER

BONUS TRIVIA

SUPPOSEDLY CREATED IN THE 1980s AFTER SOME FRIENDS IN CANADA RAN LOW ON THE STUFF TO MAKE WHITE RUSSIANS.

1 OZ
CREAM

1 OZ
VODKA

1 OZ
COFFEE
LIQUEUR

5 OZ
COCA-COLA

YOU SHOULD PROBABLY USE A HIGHBALL GLASS.

FIRST THINGS FIRST, GO BUY SOME:

■ BÉNÉDICTINE

OH, AND YOU'LL ALSO NEED A LEMON

> THERE ARE ONLY 3 PEOPLE ON EARTH WHO KNOW THE
> FULL, 27-INGREDIENT RECIPE FOR MAKING BÉNÉDICTINE.

INGREDIENTS

- 2 OZ DRY GIN
- .5 OZ SWEET VERMOUTH
- 1 TSP BÉNÉDICTINE
- 2 DASH ORANGE BITTERS
- LEMON (GARNISH)

INSTRUCTIONS

- CHILL SERVING GLASS ☐
- GET MIXING GLASS ☐
- FILL WITH ICE ☐
- ADD ALL INGREDIENTS ☐
- STIR UNTIL CHILLED ☐
- STRAIN INTO SERVING GLASS ☐
- GARNISH W/ LEMON TWIST ☐

WHAT DO YOU THINK?

. . . .

. . . .

. . . .

DRINK THIS AGAIN?   YES ☐   NO ☐   IF DESPERATE ☐

THE COSMETIC USE FOR BOTOX WAS ACCIDENTALLY DISCOV-
ERED IN 1987 BY TWO VANCOUVER DOCTORS. IT'S NOT L.A.'S
FAULT.

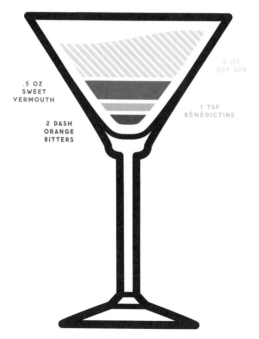

2 OZ
DRY GIN

.5 OZ
SWEET
VERMOUTH

1 TSP
BÉNÉDICTINE

2 DASH
ORANGE
BITTERS

THIS ONE DEFINITELY CALLS FOR A MARTINI GLASS.

YOU PRETTY MUCH HAVE EVERYTHING YOU NEED:

☐ SO MAKE A DRINK ALREADY

CHECK YOUR BAR FOR ANYTHING YOU'RE GETTING LOW ON, THOUGH

NAMED AFTER CANON FÉLIX KIR (MAYOR OF DIJON, FRANCE) WHO POPULARIZED THE LOCALLY MADE DRINK.

INGREDIENTS **INSTRUCTIONS**

☐ 1 OZ CRÈME DE CASSIS   CHILL SERVING GLASS ☐

☐ 5 OZ CHAMPAGNE   POUR IN CRÈME DE CASSIS ☐

TOP W/ CHAMPAGNE ☐

WHAT DO YOU THINK?

. . . .

. . . .

. . . .

. . . .

. . . .

DRINK THIS AGAIN?   YES ☐   NO ☐   IF DESPERATE ☐

5 OZ
CHAMPAGNE

1 OZ
CRÈME DE
CASSIS

FINALLY, A USE FOR THOSE CHAMPAGNE FLUTES.

YOU PRETTY MUCH HAVE EVERYTHING YOU NEED:

JUST MAKE SURE YOU HAVE SOME BLACKBERRIES

AND MAYBE CHECK THE FRESHNESS OF THAT LEMON JUICE

THE PERFECT DRINK TO TAKE THE EDGE OFF OF
THE PUN THAT YOU JUST HAD TO ENDURE.

INGREDIENTS

2 OZ VODKA
8 BLACKBERRIES
.25 OZ RASPBERRY LIQUEUR
.5 OZ LEMON JUICE
GINGER BEER
BLACKBERRY (GARNISH)

INSTRUCTIONS

GET SHAKER ☐
ADD FIRST 2 INGREDIENTS ☐
MUDDLE UNTIL MIXED ☐
FILL WITH ICE ☐
ADD NEXT 2 INGREDIENTS ☐
SHAKE UNTIL CHILLED ☐
STRAIN INTO GLASS W/ ICE ☐
TOP WITH GINGER BEER ☐
GARNISH W/ BLACKBERRY ☐

WHAT DO YOU THINK?

DRINK THIS AGAIN? YES ☐ NO ☐ IF DESPERATE ☐

BONUS TRIVIA

UK FOLKLORE SAYS THAT BLACKBERRIES CAN'T BE PICKED AFTER
OLD MICHAELMAS DAY (OCT. 11TH). THE DEVIL POISONS THEM.

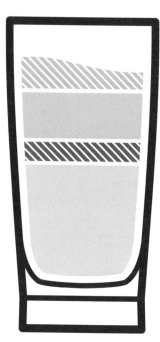

.5 OZ
LEMON
JUICE

2 OZ
VODKA

.25 OZ
RASPBERRY
LIQUEUR

GINGER
BEER

YOU SHOULD PROBABLY USE A HIGHBALL GLASS.

YOU PRETTY MUCH HAVE EVERYTHING YOU NEED:

JUST MAKE SURE YOU HAVE SOME PINEAPPLE

AND MAYBE CHECK THE FRESHNESS OF THOSE JUICES

ORIGINALLY, THE GARNISH CALLED FOR FANNING THE
LEAVES OF A PINEAPPLE TO MIMIC FEATHERS ON A BIRD.*

INGREDIENTS

- 1.5 OZ DARK RUM
- 1.5 OZ PINEAPPLE JUICE
- .75 OZ CAMPARI
- .5 OZ LIME JUICE
- .5 OZ SIMPLE SYRUP
- PINEAPPLE (GARNISH)

INSTRUCTIONS

- GET SHAKER & ADD ICE ☐
- ADD ALL INGREDIENTS ☐
- SHAKE VIGOROUSLY ☐
- GET SERVING GLASS ☐
- FILL WITH ICE ☐
- STRAIN INTO GLASS ☐
- GARNISH W/ PINEAPPLE WEDGE ☐

WHAT DO YOU THINK?

. . . .

. . . .

. . . .

*YOU CAN TOO, IF YOU REALLY WANT. WE'LL PASS.

DRINK THIS AGAIN?   YES ☐   NO ☐   IF DESPERATE ☐

BONUS TRIVIA

THIS DRINK WAS CREATED IN 1973 BY JEFFREY ONG, AT THE FORMER KUALA LUMPUR HILTON IN MALAYSIA. ARRIVING GUESTS WERE GREETED IN THE HOTEL'S 'AVIARY BAR,' WHERE THEY WERE SERVED THIS AS A WELCOME DRINK.

IT EVEN CAME IN A BIRD-SHAPED CERAMIC VESSEL.

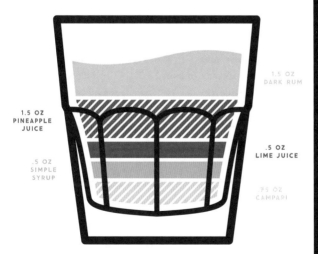

1.5 OZ
DARK RUM

1.5 OZ
PINEAPPLE
JUICE

.5 OZ
SIMPLE
SYRUP

.5 OZ
LIME JUICE

.75 OZ
CAMPARI

WE'D RECOMMEND A LOWBALL GLASS FOR THIS ONE.

FIRST THINGS FIRST, GO BUY SOME:

LEMON-LIME SODA

OH, AND YOU'LL ALSO NEED A LEMON (AND A BRANDIED CHERRY)

THIS COCKTAIL IS THE NAMESAKE OF AN AFTERSHAVE
THAT SAILORS DRANK DURING WWII FOR 'RECREATION.'

INGREDIENTS	INSTRUCTIONS
.75 OZ VODKA	GET SHAKER & ADD ICE ☐
.75 OZ DRY GIN	ADD FIRST 3 INGREDIENTS ☐
.5 OZ CURAÇAO	SHAKE UNTIL CHILLED ☐
LEMON-LIME SODA	GET SERVING GLASS ☐
BRANDIED CHERRY (GARNISH)	FILL WITH ICE ☐
LEMON (GARNISH)	STRAIN INTO GLASS ☐
	TOP W/ LEMON-LIME SODA ☐
	GARNISH W/ LEMON SLICE ☐
	ADD BRANDIED CHERRY ☐

WHAT DO YOU THINK?

....

DRINK THIS AGAIN?   YES ☐   NO ☐   IF DESPERATE ☐

BONUS TRIVIA

PORTRAYED AS THE FAVORITE DRINK OF ROBERT GRAYSMITH
(PLAYED BY JAKE GYLLENHAAL) IN THE 2007 MOVIE 'ZODIAC.'

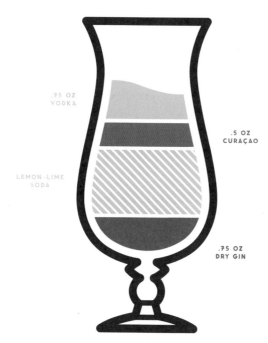

.75 OZ
VODKA

.5 OZ
CURAÇAO

LEMON-LIME
SODA

.75 OZ
DRY GIN

USE THE HURRICANE GLASS YOU STOLE ON VACATION.

FIRST THINGS FIRST, GO BUY SOME:

▮ OLIVE JUICE (NO, NOT THAT EXTRA LIQUID IN THE JAR)

OH, AND YOU'LL ALSO NEED SOME ACTUAL OLIVES TOO

ALLEGEDLY BORN OUT OF PRESIDENT FRANKLIN D.
ROOSEVELT'S INABILITY TO MAKE A GOOD MARTINI.

INGREDIENTS

INSTRUCTIONS

▮ 2.5 OZ DRY GIN

GET MIXING GLASS & ADD ICE ☐

▮ .5 OZ DRY VERMOUTH

ADD ALL INGREDIENTS ☐

▮ .5 OZ OLIVE JUICE

STIR UNTIL CHILLED ☐

▮ OLIVE (GARNISH)

STRAIN INTO SERVING GLASS ☐

GARNISH W/ OLIVE ☐

WHAT DO YOU THINK?

. . . .

. . . .

. . . .

. . . .

DRINK THIS AGAIN?   YES ☐   NO ☐   IF DESPERATE ☐

THE ONLY DIFFERENCE BETWEEN GREEN AND BLACK OLIVES
IS RIPENESS. UNRIPE OLIVES ARE GREEN. RIPE ARE BLACK.

2.5 OZ
DRY GIN

.5 OZ
OLIVE JUICE

.5 OZ DRY
VERMOUTH

THIS ONE DEFINITELY CALLS FOR A MARTINI GLASS.

YOU PRETTY MUCH HAVE EVERYTHING YOU NEED:

☐ JUST MAKE SURE YOU HAVE A BRANDIED CHERRY

CHECK YOUR BAR FOR ANYTHING YOU'RE GETTING LOW ON, THOUGH

DESPITE THIS DRINK'S NAME, CLINT REPORTEDLY
PREFERS A NICE CHARDONNAY.

INGREDIENTS

- 1.5 OZ BOURBON
- .75 OZ SWEET VERMOUTH
- 2 DASH ORANGE BITTERS
- BRANDIED CHERRY (GARNISH)

INSTRUCTIONS

GET SHAKER & ADD ICE ☐
ADD ALL INGREDIENTS ☐
SHAKE UNTIL CHILLED ☐
STRAIN INTO GLASS ☐
GARNISH W/ CHERRY ☐

WHAT DO YOU THINK?

DRINK THIS AGAIN? YES ☐ NO ☐ IF DESPERATE ☐

BONUS TRIVIA

IN 1959, HE WAS FIRED AS A CONTRACT ACTOR FOR UNIVERSAL
BECAUSE HIS ADAM'S APPLE STUCK OUT TOO FAR.

1.5 OZ
BOURBON

2 DASH
ORANGE
BITTERS

.75 OZ
SWEET
VERMOUTH

THIS ONE DEFINITELY CALLS FOR A MARTINI GLASS.

FIRST THINGS FIRST, GO BUY SOME:

AMONTILLADO SHERRY

OH, AND YOU'LL ALSO NEED A LEMON

THE 1846 EDGAR ALLAN POE STORY 'THE CASK OF AMONTILLADO' CENTERS AROUND TASTING THIS SHERRY.

INGREDIENTS

- 1.25 OZ AMONTILLADO SHERRY
- 1.25 OZ RYE WHISKEY
- .5 OZ ORANGE LIQUEUR
- 2 DASH ANGOSTURA BITTERS
- LEMON (GARNISH)

INSTRUCTIONS

- GET MIXING GLASS ☐
- FILL WITH ICE ☐
- ADD ALL INGREDIENTS ☐
- STIR UNTIL CHILLED ☐
- STRAIN INTO GLASS ☐
- GARNISH W/ LEMON TWIST ☐

WHAT DO YOU THINK?

. . . .

. . . .

. . . .

. . . .

DRINK THIS AGAIN?   YES ☐   NO ☐   IF DESPERATE ☐

BONUS TRIVIA

FIRST DOCUMENTED IN THE 1916 BOOK 'RECIPES FOR MIXED DRINKS' BY HUGO ENSSLIN – LIKELY THE LAST COCKTAIL BOOK PUBLISHED BEFORE PROHIBITION RUINED EVERYTHING.

1.25 OZ RYE WHISKEY

.5 OZ ORANGE LIQUEUR

2 DASH ANGOSTURA BITTERS

1.25 OZ AMONTILLADO SHERRY

USE A COUPE GLASS. TRUST US, IT'S WORTH IT.

YOU PRETTY MUCH HAVE EVERYTHING YOU NEED:

JUST MAKE SURE YOU HAVE A LEMON

OH, AND YOU'LL ALSO NEED AN ORANGE TOO

A DANDY IS A MAN WHO IS EXCESSIVELY CONCERNED
WITH HOW HE LOOKS. IT'S THE PERFECT 1800s BURN.

INGREDIENTS   INSTRUCTIONS

INGREDIENTS	INSTRUCTIONS
1.5 OZ RYE WHISKEY	GET MIXING GLASS ☐
1.5 OZ DUBONNET ROUGE	FILL WITH ICE ☐
1 DASH ANGOSTURA BITTERS	ADD ALL INGREDIENTS ☐
1 TSP TRIPLE SEC	STIR UNTIL CHILLED ☐
LEMON (GARNISH)	STRAIN INTO SERVING GLASS ☐
ORANGE (GARNISH)	GARNISH W/ LEMON TWIST ☐
	ADD AN ORANGE TWIST ☐

WHAT DO YOU THINK?

. . . .

. . . .

DRINK THIS AGAIN?   YES ☐   NO ☐   IF DESPERATE ☐

BONUS TRIVIA

DUBONNET IS AN AROMATIZED WINE, SO IT WILL EVENTUALLY SPOIL. JUST BE SURE TO REFRIGERATE IT AFTER OPENING...AND GET A NEW BOTTLE AFTER 2 MONTHS OR SO.

1.5 OZ
RYE
WHISKEY

1 TSP
TRIPLE SEC

1 DASH
ANGOSTURA
BITTERS

1.5 OZ
DUBONNET
ROUGE

USE A COUPE GLASS. TRUST US, IT'S WORTH IT.

FIRST THINGS FIRST, GO BUY SOME:

▓ AMARETTO

DON'T FORGET TO ADD THIS TO YOUR INVENTORY LIST

ORIGINALLY MADE FROM BITTER ALMONDS, AMARETTO
IS, IN FACT, ITALIAN FOR 'A LITTLE BITTER.'

INGREDIENTS	INSTRUCTIONS
▓ 2 OZ SCOTCH	GET SERVING GLASS & ADD ICE ☐
▓ 2 OZ AMARETTO	ADD BOTH INGREDIENTS ☐
	STIR TO COMBINE ☐

WHAT DO YOU THINK?

. . . .

. . . .

. . . .

. . . .

. . . .

. . . .

DRINK THIS AGAIN?   YES ☐   NO ☐   IF DESPERATE ☐

BONUS TRIVIA

IN ORDER TO SAVE COSTS, PARAMOUNT ASKED FRANCIS FORD
COPPOLA TO MODERNIZE THE SCRIPT FOR 'THE GODFATHER' SO
THAT IT TOOK PLACE IN PRESENT DAY (WHICH WAS 1972), AND
SHOOT THE FILM IN KANSAS CITY INSTEAD OF NEW YORK.
HE DECLINED.

SIDE NOTE: WE'RE ALSO NOT SURE WHAT THAT SAYS ABOUT
KANSAS CITY IN THE 70s.

2 OZ
SCOTCH

2 OZ
AMARETTO

WE'D RECOMMEND A LOWBALL GLASS FOR THIS ONE.

YOU PRETTY MUCH HAVE EVERYTHING YOU NEED:

JUST MAKE SURE YOU HAVE A LIME

AND MAYBE CHECK THE FRESHNESS OF THOSE JUICES

FRESH CRANBERRY JUICE IS JUST WAY TOO TART TO
WORK WITH. SO, FOR ONCE, USE THE BOTTLED STUFF.

INGREDIENTS

- 1.5 OZ VODKA
- 1.5 OZ GRAPEFRUIT JUICE
- 3 OZ CRANBERRY JUICE
- LIME (GARNISH)

INSTRUCTIONS

GET SERVING GLASS ☐
FILL WITH ICE ☐
ADD ALL INGREDIENTS ☐
STIR UNTIL CHILLED ☐
GARNISH W/ LIME SLICE ☐

WHAT DO YOU THINK?

. . . .

. . . .

. . . .

DRINK THIS AGAIN? YES ☐ NO ☐ IF DESPERATE ☐

BONUS TRIVIA

CRANBERRIES AREN'T ACTUALLY GROWN IN WATER. BUT SINCE THEY FLOAT, THEIR BOGS ARE FLOODED TO HARVEST THEM.

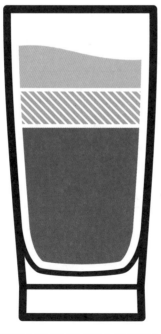

1.5 OZ
VODKA

1.5 OZ
GRAPEFRUIT
JUICE

3 OZ
CRANBERRY
JUICE

YOU SHOULD PROBABLY USE A HIGHBALL GLASS.

YOU PRETTY MUCH HAVE EVERYTHING YOU NEED:

JUST MAKE SURE YOU HAVE AN ORANGE

CHECK YOUR BAR FOR ANYTHING YOU'RE GETTING LOW ON, THOUGH

IT WAS REPORTEDLY A FAVORITE AT THE 'AMERICAN BAR' ON THE SS EUROPA (A 1930s GERMAN OCEAN LINER).

INGREDIENTS

2 OZ DRY VERMOUTH

.75 OZ BÉNÉDICTINE

3 DASH ABSINTHE

ORANGE (GARNISH)

INSTRUCTIONS

CHILL SERVING GLASS ☐

GET MIXING GLASS & ADD ICE ☐

ADD ALL INGREDIENTS ☐

STIR UNTIL CHILLED ☐

STRAIN INTO GLASS ☐

GARNISH W/ ORANGE TWIST ☐

WHAT DO YOU THINK?

. . . .

. . . .

. . . .

DRINK THIS AGAIN?   YES ☐   NO ☐   IF DESPERATE ☐

BONUS TRIVIA

THE CHRYSANTHEMUM GETS ITS NAME FROM THE GREEK WORDS
'CHRYSOS' (MEANING GOLD) AND 'ANTHOS' (MEANING FLOWER).

2 OZ DRY
VERMOUTH

3 DASH
ABSINTHE

.75 OZ
BÉNÉDICTINE

THIS ONE DEFINITELY CALLS FOR A MARTINI GLASS.

YOU PRETTY MUCH HAVE EVERYTHING YOU NEED:

JUST MAKE SURE YOU HAVE AN EGG HANDY

OH, AND YOU'LL ALSO NEED A BRANDIED CHERRY

A FAVORITE OF AZIZ ANSARI. HE RECOMMENDS POURING IT OVER 'THE BIGGEST ICE CUBE YOU CAN FIND.'*

INGREDIENTS	INSTRUCTIONS
1.5 OZ BOURBON	GET SHAKER & FILL W/ ICE ☐
.75 OZ LEMON JUICE	ADD ALL INGREDIENTS ☐
.75 OZ HONEY SYRUP	SHAKE UNTIL CHILLED ☐
1 EGG WHITE	GET SERVING GLASS ☐
BRANDIED CHERRY (GARNISH)	*ADD ICE CUBE ☐
	STRAIN INTO GLASS ☐
	GARNISH W/ CHERRY ☐

WHAT DO YOU THINK?

. . . .

. . . .

. . . .

DRINK THIS AGAIN?   YES ☐   NO ☐   IF DESPERATE ☐

BONUS TRIVIA

THE SIGNATURE MEAL OF THE GOLD RUSH WAS CALLED THE 'HANGTOWN FRY,' WHICH CONSISTED OF A FRIED EGG SITTING ATOP AN OYSTER COVERED IN BACON. THIS DISH WAS SAID TO HAVE BEEN CREATED IN 1850 WHEN A GOLD PROSPECTOR WHO STRUCK IT RICH WALKED INTO A RESTAURANT IN THE TOWN OF HANGTOWN (NOW PLACERVILLE, CA) AND DEMANDED THE MOST EXPENSIVE DISH THE RESTAURANT COULD MAKE.

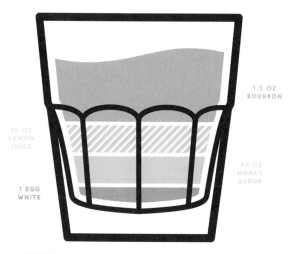

1.5 OZ
BOURBON

.75 OZ
LEMON
JUICE

.75 OZ
HONEY
SYRUP

1 EGG
WHITE

WE'D RECOMMEND A LOWBALL GLASS FOR THIS ONE.

MAKE A FROSECCO

FIRST THINGS FIRST, GO BUY SOME:

ELDERFLOWER LIQUEUR

OH, AND YOU'LL NEED A STRAW TO DRINK THIS WITH

WHAT CAN WE SAY? IT'S BASICALLY A BOOZE SLUSHIE.
THEY CAN'T ALL BE REFINED & SOPHISTICATED.

INGREDIENTS	INSTRUCTIONS
PROSECCO (FOR ICE CUBES)	GET ICE CUBE TRAY ☐
1 OZ LEMON JUICE	FILL W/ PROSECCO ☐
1 OZ ELDERFLOWER LIQUEUR	WAIT UNTIL FROZEN ☐
2 OZ PROSECCO	GET BLENDER ☐
	ADD 6 PROSECCO CUBES ☐
	ADD NEXT 2 INGREDIENTS ☐
	PULSE BLEND UNTIL SLUSHY ☐
	ADD PROSECCO & BLEND AGAIN ☐
	POUR INTO SERVING GLASS ☐

WHAT DO YOU THINK?

. . . .

DRINK THIS AGAIN?   YES ☐   NO ☐   IF DESPERATE ☐

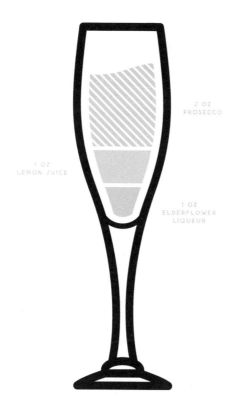

2 OZ
PROSECCO

1 OZ
LEMON JUICE

1 OZ
ELDERFLOWER
LIQUEUR

FINALLY, A USE FOR THOSE CHAMPAGNE FLUTES.

YOU PRETTY MUCH HAVE EVERYTHING YOU NEED:

■ JUST MAKE SURE YOU HAVE AN ORANGE

CHECK YOUR BAR FOR ANYTHING YOU'RE GETTING LOW ON, THOUGH

LIKELY NAMED AFTER GENERAL GERARDO MACHADO,
THE PRESIDENT OF CUBA AT THE TIME (1925 TO 1933).

INGREDIENTS

- 1.5 OZ WHITE RUM
- .75 OZ DRY VERMOUTH
- .5 OZ CURAÇAO
- 1 DASH GRENADINE
- ORANGE (GARNISH)

INSTRUCTIONS

- CHILL SERVING GLASS ☐
- GET SHAKER & FILL W/ ICE ☐
- ADD ALL INGREDIENTS ☐
- SHAKE UNTIL CHILLED ☐
- STRAIN INTO SERVING GLASS ☐
- GARNISH W/ ORANGE TWIST ☐

WHAT DO YOU THINK?

. . . .

. . . .

. . . .

DRINK THIS AGAIN?   YES ☐   NO ☐   IF DESPERATE ☐

BONUS TRIVIA

PRESIDENT MACHADO GAVE PAN AMERICAN AIRWAYS EXCLUSIVE
RIGHTS TO FLY THE FLORIDA-HAVANA ROUTE. PAN-AM LATER
SERVED A VARIATION OF THIS DRINK ON THEIR LARGER PLANES.
COINCIDENCE?

1.5 OZ
WHITE
RUM

1 DASH
GRENADINE

.5 OZ
CURAÇAO

.75 OZ
DRY VERMOUTH

USE A COUPE GLASS. TRUST US, IT'S WORTH IT.

YOU PRETTY MUCH HAVE EVERYTHING YOU NEED:

☐ JUST MAKE SURE YOU HAVE A LIME

CHECK YOUR BAR FOR ANYTHING YOU'RE GETTING LOW ON, THOUGH

CREATED IN 1945 BY THE OCEAN SPRAY CRANBERRY GROWER'S CO-OP. WOW, WAY TO BE CREATIVE, GUYS.

INGREDIENTS

☐ 1.5 OZ VODKA
☐ CRANBERRY JUICE
☐ LIME (GARNISH)

INSTRUCTIONS

GET SERVING GLASS ☐
FILL WITH ICE & ADD VODKA ☐
TOP W/ CRANBERRY JUICE ☐
STIR UNTIL CHILLED ☐
GARNISH W/ LIME WEDGE ☐

WHAT DO YOU THINK?

. . . .

. . . .

. . . .

. . . .

DRINK THIS AGAIN?   YES ☐   NO ☐   IF DESPERATE ☐

BONUS TRIVIA

FULLY RIPE CRANBERRIES BOUNCE, AND MUST CLEAR A 4" TALL
BOARD DURING HARVESTING TO SORT OUT THE BAD ONES.

CRANBERRY
JUICE

1.5 OZ
VODKA

YOU SHOULD PROBABLY USE A HIGHBALL GLASS.

FIRST THINGS FIRST, GO BUY SOME:

☐ PEACH PUREE (THEY MAKE IT JUST FOR COCKTAILS)

YOU CAN ALSO MAKE SOME FROM CANNED PEACHES (WE'RE LAZY)

THIS DRINK'S RESEMBLANCE TO A PINK TOGA IN A
PAINTING BY GIOVANNI BELLINI INSPIRED ITS NAME.

INGREDIENTS	INSTRUCTIONS
☐ 2 OZ PEACH PUREE	CHILL SERVING GLASS ☐
☐ 4 OZ PROSECCO	ADD BOTH INGREDIENTS ☐
	STIR GENTLY ☐

WHAT DO YOU THINK?

. . . .

. . . .

. . . .

. . . .

. . . .

DRINK THIS AGAIN?　　　YES ☐　　NO ☐　　IF DESPERATE ☐

MAKE A BELLINI

4 OZ
PROSECCO

2 OZ
PEACH PUREE

FINALLY, A USE FOR THOSE CHAMPAGNE FLUTES.

MAKE A RED HOOK

YOU PRETTY MUCH HAVE EVERYTHING YOU NEED:

■ JUST MAKE SURE YOU HAVE SOME BRANDIED CHERRIES

CHECK YOUR BAR FOR ANYTHING YOU'RE GETTING LOW ON, THOUGH

CREATED IN 2003 BY VINCENZO ERRICO AT THE FAMOUS
'MILK & HONEY' BAR IN NYC (SADLY, NOW CLOSED).

INGREDIENTS	INSTRUCTIONS
■ 2 OZ RYE WHISKEY	GET MIXING GLASS ☐
■ .5 OZ MARASCHINO LIQUEUR	FILL WITH ICE ☐
■ .5 OZ SWEET VERMOUTH	ADD ALL INGREDIENTS ☐
■ BRANDIED CHERRY (GARNISH)	STIR UNTIL CHILLED ☐
	STRAIN INTO GLASS ☐
	GARNISH W/ CHERRY ☐

WHAT DO YOU THINK?

. . . .

. . . .

. . . .

DRINK THIS AGAIN?   YES ☐   NO ☐   IF DESPERATE ☐

MAKE A RED HOOK

THE RED HOOK AREA OF BROOKLYN, NY, WAS FIRST SETTLED IN 1636, AND NAMED FOR ITS RED CLAY SOIL AND HOOK-SHAPED PENINSULA THAT JUTS INTO THE EAST RIVER.

2 OZ
RYE
WHISKEY

.5 OZ
SWEET
VERMOUTH

.5 OZ
MARASCHINO
LIQUEUR

USE A COUPE GLASS. TRUST US, IT'S WORTH IT.

YOU PRETTY MUCH HAVE EVERYTHING YOU NEED:

◼ JUST MAKE SURE YOU HAVE SOME BLACK LICORICE

◼ AND MAYBE PICK UP A FRESH CAN OF COKE WHILE YOU'RE AT IT

> THE GLYCYRRHIZIN ACID EXTRACTED FROM LICORICE
> ROOT IS 30 TO 50 TIMES SWEETER THAN TABLE SUGAR.

INGREDIENTS

◼ 4 OZ COCA-COLA

◼ 1.75 OZ ANISETTE LIQUEUR

◼ BLACK LICORICE (GARNISH)

INSTRUCTIONS

GET SERVING GLASS ☐

FILL WITH ICE ☐

ADD ALL INGREDIENTS ☐

STIR UNTIL CHILLED ☐

GARNISH W/ LICORICE STICK ☐

WHAT DO YOU THINK?

. . . .

. . . .

. . . .

. . . .

DRINK THIS AGAIN?   YES ☐   NO ☐   IF DESPERATE ☐

THE LICORICE PLANT IS ALSO USED TO MANUFACTURE THE
FOAM INSIDE OF FIRE EXTINGUISHERS.

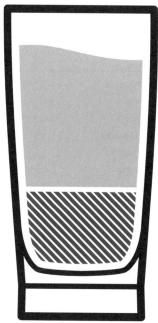

4 OZ
COCA-COLA

1.75 OZ
ANISETTE
LIQUEUR

YOU SHOULD PROBABLY USE A HIGHBALL GLASS.

FIRST THINGS FIRST, GO BUY SOME:

TOMATO JUICE

OH, AND YOU'LL ALSO NEED OLIVES, A CUCUMBER, AND SOME PEPPER

MOSQUITOES PREFER TYPE O BLOOD, & LAND ON THOSE
THAT HAVE IT TWICE AS OFTEN AS PEOPLE W/ TYPE A.

INGREDIENTS

INSTRUCTIONS

INGREDIENTS	INSTRUCTIONS
3 OZ BLANCO TEQUILA	GET SHAKER & ADD ICE ☐
.5 OZ LIME JUICE	ADD ALL INGREDIENTS ☐
6 OZ TOMATO JUICE	SHAKE UNTIL CHILLED ☐
4 DASH TABASCO SAUCE	GET SERVING GLASS ☐
1 PINCH BLACK PEPPER	ADD LIGHT ICE ☐
2 TSP OLIVE JUICE	STRAIN INTO GLASS ☐
2 OLIVES (GARNISH)	GARNISH W/ OLIVES ☐
CUCUMBER (GARNISH)	ADD CUCUMBER SLICE ☐

WHAT DO YOU THINK?

. . . .

. . . .

DRINK THIS AGAIN?   YES ☐   NO ☐   IF DESPERATE ☐

THE UBIQUITOUS CELERY GARNISH WAS BORN WHEN, WITHOUT
A STIR STICK, A CUSTOMER IMPROVISED W/ A STICK OF IT.

6 OZ
TOMATO
JUICE

1 PINCH
BLACK
PEPPER

.5 OZ
LIME JUICE

4 DASH
TABASCO
SAUCE

2 TSP
OLIVE
JUICE

3 OZ
BLANCO
TEQUILA

YOU SHOULD PROBABLY USE A HIGHBALL GLASS.

FIRST THINGS FIRST, GO BUY SOME:

■ ORANGE FLOWER WATER

OH, AND YOU'LL ALSO NEED AN EGG

YOU'LL BE DRY SHAKING (NO ICE) FOR 10 SECONDS,
AND SHAKING AGAIN W/ ICE FOR 15 SECONDS. HARD.

INGREDIENTS	INSTRUCTIONS
2 OZ DRY GIN	GET SHAKER ☐
.75 OZ SIMPLE SYRUP	ADD FIRST 7 INGREDIENTS ☐
.5 OZ CREAM	DRY SHAKE VIGOROUSLY ☐
.5 OZ LEMON JUICE	ADD ICE AND SHAKE AGAIN ☐
.5 OZ LIME JUICE	GET SERVING GLASS ☐
3 DASH ORANGE FLOWER WATER	STRAIN INTO GLASS ☐
1 EGG WHITE	TOP W/ CLUB SODA ☐
CLUB SODA	

WHAT DO YOU THINK?

. . . .

. . . .

DRINK THIS AGAIN? YES ☐ NO ☐ IF DESPERATE ☐

BONUS TRIVIA

WHILE FIRST KNOWN AS THE NEW ORLEANS FIZZ, THIS DRINK
BECAME SO POPULAR AFTER ITS CREATION IN 1888 THAT IT
EVENTUALLY TOOK ON THE NAME OF ITS INVENTOR,
HENRY C. RAMOS.

IN FACT, IT WAS SUCH A SUCCESS THAT RAMO'S BAR IN NEW
ORLEANS HAD TO EMPLOY 20 ADDITIONAL BARTENDERS FULL
TIME, ALL WORKING SOLELY ON MAKING THIS COCKTAIL.

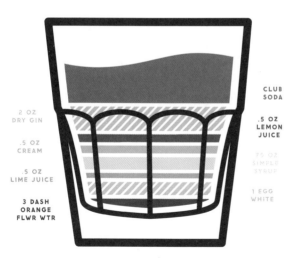

2 OZ
DRY GIN

.5 OZ
CREAM

.5 OZ
LIME JUICE

3 DASH
ORANGE
FLWR WTR

CLUB
SODA

.5 OZ
LEMON
JUICE

.75 OZ
SIMPLE
SYRUP

1 EGG
WHITE

WE'D RECOMMEND A LOWBALL GLASS FOR THIS ONE.

YOU PRETTY MUCH HAVE EVERYTHING YOU NEED:

■ JUST MAKE SURE YOU HAVE SOME BRANDIED CHERRIES

OH, AND YOU'LL ALSO NEED AN EGG

THIS IS AN ELEVATED VERSION OF THE 'CLASSIC,' AND BY CLASSIC, WE MEAN YOUR GRANDMA LOVED THEM.

INGREDIENTS

- 1.5 OZ AMARETTO LIQUEUR
- .75 OZ BOURBON
- 1 OZ LEMON JUICE
- 1 TSP SIMPLE SYRUP
- .5 OZ EGG WHITE
- BRANDIED CHERRY (GARNISH)

INSTRUCTIONS

- GET SHAKER ☐
- ADD ALL INGREDIENTS ☐
- DRY SHAKE UNTIL MIXED ☐
- ADD ICE & SHAKE AGAIN ☐
- GET SERVING GLASS ☐
- STRAIN INTO GLASS ☐
- GARNISH W/ CHERRY ☐

WHAT DO YOU THINK?

. . . .

. . . .

. . . .

DRINK THIS AGAIN?   YES ☐   NO ☐   IF DESPERATE ☐

BONUS TRIVIA

IN 2011, METHOD MAN RELEASED THE SONG 'WORLD GONE SOUR'
AT THE REQUEST OF THE COMPANY BEHIND SOUR PATCH KIDS.

1.5 OZ
AMARETTO

1 TSP
SIMPLE SYRUP

1 OZ
LEMON JUICE

.75 OZ
BOURBON

.5 OZ
EGG WHITE

THIS ONE LOOKS GREAT IN A MARTINI GLASS.

MAKE A CASSIS SPRITZ

YOU PRETTY MUCH HAVE EVERYTHING YOU NEED:

☐ JUST MAKE SURE YOU HAVE SOME BLACKBERRIES

CHECK YOUR BAR FOR ANYTHING YOU'RE GETTING LOW ON, THOUGH

> A GREAT ALTERNATIVE TO SANGRIA IF YOU DON'T HAVE
> THE TIME TO CHOP FRUIT (OR, LIKE, EVEN HAVE FRUIT).

INGREDIENTS

- 4 OZ PROSECCO
- 1 OZ CRÈME DE CASSIS
- CLUB SODA
- 2 BLACKBERRIES (GARNISH)

INSTRUCTIONS

- GET SERVING GLASS ☐
- FILL WITH ICE ☐
- ADD FIRST 2 INGREDIENTS ☐
- TOP W/ CLUB SODA ☐
- STIR TO COMBINE ☐
- GARNISH W/ BLACKBERRIES ☐

WHAT DO YOU THINK?

. . . .

. . . .

. . . .

DRINK THIS AGAIN?   YES ☐   NO ☐   IF DESPERATE ☐

MAKE A CASSIS SPRITZ

CRÈME DE CASSIS IS MADE FROM BLACKCURRANT BERRIES.

CLUB SODA

4 OZ
PROSECCO

1 OZ
CRÈME DE
CASSIS

USE A WINE GLASS, YOU'LL FEEL EXTRA FANCY.

FIRST THINGS FIRST, GO BUY SOME:

- WORCESTERSHIRE SAUCE (IT'S $\overline{\text{WU}}$-STUH-SHR BY THE WAY)

OH, AND MAKE SURE YOU HAVE AN EGG TOO

THOUGH CONSIDERED TO BE AN OLD HANGOVER REMEDY, HEADACHE EXPERTS DISAGREE (AND APPARENTLY EXIST).

INGREDIENTS   **INSTRUCTIONS**

INGREDIENTS	INSTRUCTIONS
1.5 OZ COGNAC	GET SHAKER & ADD ICE ☐
.25 OZ TOMATO JUICE	ADD FIRST 4 INGREDIENTS ☐
.25 OZ WORCESTERSHIRE S.	SHAKE UNTIL CHILLED ☐
1 DASH TABASCO SAUCE	STRAIN INTO GLASS ☐
1 WHOLE EGG YOLK	TOP WITH YOLK ☐

WHAT DO YOU THINK?

. . . .

. . . .

. . . .

. . . .

DRINK THIS AGAIN?   YES ☐   NO ☐   IF DESPERATE ☐

BONUS TRIVIA

A SINGLE OYSTER CAN FILTER AN AVERAGE OF 50 GALLONS OF WATER A DAY. THEY'RE A TRIPLE THREAT: THEY MAKE WATER CLEARER, REMOVE POLLUTANTS...AND TASTE DELICIOUS.

1.5 OZ
COGNAC

.25 OZ
TOMATO
JUICE

1 WHOLE
EGG YOLK

1 DASH
TABASCO
SAUCE

.25 OZ
WORCESTERSHIRE
SAUCE

USE A COUPE GLASS. TRUST US, IT'S WORTH IT.

YOU PRETTY MUCH HAVE EVERYTHING YOU NEED:

☐ JUST MAKE SURE YOU HAVE SOME BRANDIED CHERRIES

CHECK YOUR BAR FOR ANYTHING YOU'RE GETTING LOW ON. THOUGH

CREATED BY ERSKINE GWYNNE, AN AMERICAN WRITER
WHO FOUNDED THE 'BOULEVARDIER' MAGAZINE IN PARIS.

INGREDIENTS	INSTRUCTIONS
1 OZ BOURBON	GET MIXING GLASS ☐
1 OZ SWEET VERMOUTH	FILL WITH ICE ☐
1 OZ CAMPARI	ADD ALL INGREDIENTS ☐
BRANDIED CHERRY (GARNISH)	STIR UNTIL CHILLED ☐
	GET SERVING GLASS ☐
	FILL WITH ICE ☐
	STRAIN INTO GLASS ☐
	GARNISH W/ CHERRY ☐

WHAT DO YOU THINK?

. . . .

. . . .

DRINK THIS AGAIN?   YES ☐   NO ☐   IF DESPERATE ☐

BONUS TRIVIA

THE WORD BOULEVARDIER BROADLY TRANSLATES TO MEAN A 'MAN-ABOUT-TOWN.' THE FIRST BOULEVARDIERS GOT THEIR NAME FROM THE THOROUGHFARES THEY FREQUENTED...SPECIFICALLY, THE BOULEVARDS OF PARIS.

EVENTUALLY, THE TERM GREW TO REFER TO ANY WORLDLY AND SOCIALLY ACTIVE MAN. NOW WE JUST CALL THEM 'SOCIAL INFLUENCERS,' AND THEY TAKE LOTS OF PHOTOS OF LATTES.

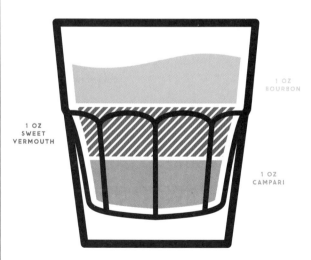

1 OZ
BOURBON

1 OZ
SWEET
VERMOUTH

1 OZ
CAMPARI

WE'D RECOMMEND A LOWBALL GLASS FOR THIS ONE.

FIRST THINGS FIRST, GO BUY SOME:

☐ FERNET (IT'S PRONOUNCED F̄UR-NUHT, WHO KNEW?)

DON'T FORGET TO ADD THIS TO YOUR INVENTORY LIST

35 PERCENT OF ALL FERNET BOTTLES IMPORTED TO THE UNITED STATES ARE CONSUMED IN SAN FRANCISCO.

INGREDIENTS

- 2 OZ RYE WHISKEY
- .75 OZ SWEET VERMOUTH
- .25 OZ FERNET

INSTRUCTIONS

GET MIXING GLASS ☐
FILL WITH ICE ☐
ADD ALL INGREDIENTS ☐
STIR UNTIL CHILLED ☐
STRAIN INTO GLASS ☐

WHAT DO YOU THINK?

. . . .

. . . .

. . . .

. . . .

DRINK THIS AGAIN?   YES ☐   NO ☐   IF DESPERATE ☐

IT'S NAMED AFTER FRANCESCO FANCIULLI, THE OVERSHADOWED
SUCCESSOR OF JOHN PHILIP SOUSA AS DIRECTOR OF THE UNITED
STATES MARINE BAND. IT'S BITTER, JUST LIKE HE WAS.

2 OZ
RYE
WHISKEY

.75 OZ
SWEET
VERMOUTH

.25 OZ
FERNET

USE A COUPE GLASS. TRUST US, IT'S WORTH IT.

YOU PRETTY MUCH HAVE EVERYTHING YOU NEED:

JUST PICK UP SOME LEMON SORBET

OH, AND YOU'LL ALSO NEED SOME MINT

IN THE VENETIAN DIALECT, SGROPPINO MEANS 'TO UNTIE A KNOT.' SPECIFICALLY, ONE IN YOUR STOMACH.

INGREDIENTS	INSTRUCTIONS
3 OZ PROSECCO	GET MIXING GLASS ☐
1 OZ VODKA	SCOOP IN SORBET ☐
1 SCOOP LEMON SORBET	ADD DASH PROSECCO ☐
2 MINT LEAVES (GARNISH)	WHISK UNTIL MIXED ☐
	WHILE WHISKING:
	ADD VODKA & PROSECCO ☐
	POUR INTO SERVING GLASS ☐
	GARNISH W/ MINT ☐

WHAT DO YOU THINK?

. . . .

. . . .

DRINK THIS AGAIN?   YES ☐   NO ☐   IF DESPERATE ☐

MAKE A SGROPPINO

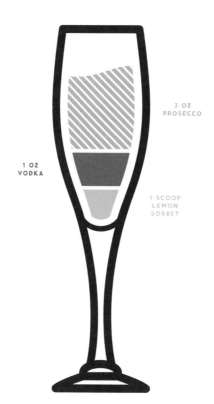

3 OZ
PROSECCO

1 OZ
VODKA

1 SCOOP
LEMON
SORBET

FINALLY, A USE FOR THOSE CHAMPAGNE FLUTES.

MAKE A CAMERON'S KICK

FIRST THINGS FIRST, GO BUY SOME:

☐ IRISH WHISKEY

AND MAYBE CHECK THE FRESHNESS OF THAT LEMON JUICE

NO ONE REALLY KNOWS WHO CAMERON IS, OR
WHAT EXACTLY HE'S TRYING TO KICK.

INGREDIENTS

- 1 OZ IRISH WHISKEY
- 1 OZ SCOTCH
- .5 OZ ORGEAT
- .5 OZ LEMON JUICE

INSTRUCTIONS

GET SHAKER & ADD ICE ☐
ADD ALL INGREDIENTS ☐
SHAKE UNTIL CHILLED ☐
GET SERVING GLASS ☐
FILL WITH ICE ☐
STRAIN INTO GLASS ☐

WHAT DO YOU THINK?

. . . .

. . . .

. . . .

DRINK THIS AGAIN? YES ☐ NO ☐ IF DESPERATE ☐

BONUS TRIVIA

TYPICALLY OTHER WHISKEYS ARE ONLY DISTILLED TWICE, WHILE
IRISH WHISKEY IS DISTILLED THREE TIMES. RIVETING, WE KNOW.

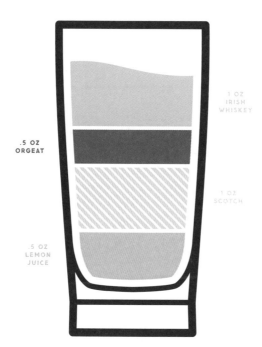

1 OZ
IRISH
WHISKEY

.5 OZ
ORGEAT

1 OZ
SCOTCH

.5 OZ
LEMON
JUICE

YOU SHOULD PROBABLY USE A HIGHBALL GLASS.

YOU PRETTY MUCH HAVE EVERYTHING YOU NEED:

☐ JUST MAKE SURE YOU HAVE A STRAWBERRY

CHECK YOUR BAR FOR ANYTHING YOU'RE GETTING LOW ON, THOUGH

> SOPHIE GERMAIN WAS A SELF-TAUGHT MATHEMATICAL GENIUS. IT'S NOT NAMED AFTER HER, BUT IT SHOULD BE.*

INGREDIENTS	INSTRUCTIONS
.75 OZ DRY GIN	GET SHAKER ☐
.5 OZ ELDERFLOWER LIQUEUR	ADD STRAWBERRY ☐
.5 OZ LEMON JUICE	MUDDLE TO MASH ☐
3 OZ CHAMPAGNE	FILL WITH ICE ☐
1 STRAWBERRY	ADD ALL LIQUIDS ☐
	SHAKE UNTIL CHILLED ☐
	STRAIN INTO GLASS ☐

WHAT DO YOU THINK?

. . . .

. . . .

. . . .

*SHE DESERVES MORE THAN THIS LITTLE BOX. LOOK HER UP.

DRINK THIS AGAIN?   YES ☐   NO ☐   IF DESPERATE ☐

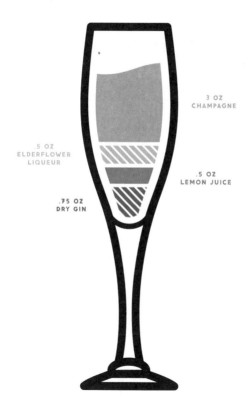

3 OZ
CHAMPAGNE

.5 OZ
ELDERFLOWER
LIQUEUR

.5 OZ
LEMON JUICE

.75 OZ
DRY GIN

FINALLY, A USE FOR THOSE CHAMPAGNE FLUTES.

YOU PRETTY MUCH HAVE EVERYTHING YOU NEED:

JUST MAKE SURE YOU HAVE AN ORANGE

AND MAYBE CHECK THE FRESHNESS OF THAT ORANGE JUICE

IF THEY'RE TRYING TO SAY THAT THE DEVIL IS A CAT,
WELL, THAT SEEMS LIKE A VALID HYPOTHESIS.

INGREDIENTS	INSTRUCTIONS
1 OZ DRY GIN	CHILL SERVING GLASS ☐
1 OZ ORANGE JUICE	GET SHAKER & FILL W/ ICE ☐
.5 OZ DRY VERMOUTH	ADD ALL INGREDIENTS ☐
.5 OZ SWEET VERMOUTH	SHAKE UNTIL CHILLED ☐
.5 OZ ORANGE LIQUEUR	STRAIN INTO GLASS ☐
1 DASH ORANGE BITTERS	GARNISH W/ ORANGE TWIST ☐
ORANGE (GARNISH)	

WHAT DO YOU THINK?

. . . .

. . . .

. . . .

DRINK THIS AGAIN?   YES ☐   NO ☐   IF DESPERATE ☐

TYPICALLY, CAT WHISKERS ARE AS LONG AS A CAT IS WIDE. THEY HELP THEM GAUGE IF THEY CAN FIT THROUGH SMALL OPENINGS.

.5 OZ ORANGE LIQUEUR

1 OZ ORANGE JUICE

1 DASH ORANGE BITTERS

1 OZ DRY GIN

.5 OZ DRY VERMOUTH

.5 OZ SWEET VERMOUTH

THIS ONE DEFINITELY CALLS FOR A MARTINI GLASS.

FIRST THINGS FIRST, GO BUY SOME:

GREEN CHARTREUSE

AND MAYBE CHECK THE FRESHNESS OF THAT LIME JUICE

BEFORE HIS DEATH IN 1977, ELVIS PRESLEY'S LAST
WORDS WERE 'I'M GOING TO THE BATHROOM TO READ.'

INGREDIENTS

.75 OZ DRY GIN
.75 OZ GREEN CHARTREUSE
.75 OZ MARASCHINO LIQUEUR
.75 OZ LIME JUICE

INSTRUCTIONS

CHILL SERVING GLASS ☐
GET SHAKER ☐
FILL WITH ICE ☐
ADD ALL INGREDIENTS ☐
SHAKE UNTIL CHILLED ☐
STRAIN INTO GLASS ☐

WHAT DO YOU THINK?

. . . .

. . . .

. . . .

. . . .

DRINK THIS AGAIN?   YES ☐   NO ☐   IF DESPERATE ☐

.75 OZ
DRY GIN

.75 OZ
GREEN
CHARTREUSE

.75 OZ
MARASCHINO
LIQUEUR

.75 OZ
LIME JUICE

USE A COUPE GLASS. TRUST US, IT'S WORTH IT.

YOU PRETTY MUCH HAVE EVERYTHING YOU NEED:

JUST MAKE SURE YOUR ORANGE JUICE IS STILL FRESH

OH, AND YOU'LL ALSO NEED AN ORANGE

THE NAME REFERS TO PEACHES (PEACH FUZZ) & NAVEL ORANGES. NOT HAIRY BELLY BUTTONS.

INGREDIENTS

3 OZ PEACH LIQUEUR
3 OZ ORANGE JUICE
ORANGE (GARNISH)

INSTRUCTIONS

GET SERVING GLASS ☐
ADD ICE & INGREDIENTS ☐
STIR BRIEFLY ☐
GARNISH W/ ORANGE TWIST ☐

WHAT DO YOU THINK?

. . . .

. . . .

. . . .

. . . .

DRINK THIS AGAIN?   YES ☐   NO ☐   IF DESPERATE ☐

BONUS TRIVIA

CREATED IN THE 1980s BY (BARTENDER, FORMER MARINE, AND PAST JOKE WRITER FOR JOHNNY CARSON) RAY FOLEY.

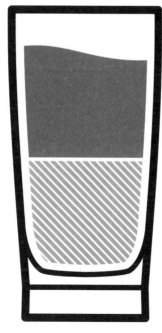

3 OZ
ORANGE
JUICE

3 OZ
PEACH
LIQUEUR

YOU SHOULD PROBABLY USE A HIGHBALL GLASS.

YOU PRETTY MUCH HAVE EVERYTHING YOU NEED:

☐ JUST MAKE SURE YOU HAVE AN EXTRA LIME

CHECK YOUR BAR FOR ANYTHING YOU'RE GETTING LOW ON, THOUGH

BAJA CALIFORNIA IS A STATE IN MEXICO. NEW MEXICO IS A STATE IN THE U.S. NEITHER FACT *SHOULD* BE TRIVIA.

INGREDIENTS

- ☐ 2 OZ REPOSADO TEQUILA
- ☐ .75 OZ PINEAPPLE JUICE
- ☐ .5 OZ AGAVE NECTAR
- ☐ LIME (GARNISH)

INSTRUCTIONS

CHILL SERVING GLASS ☐
GET SHAKER & ADD ICE ☐
ADD ALL INGREDIENTS ☐
SHAKE UNTIL CHILLED ☐
STRAIN INTO GLASS ☐
GARNISH W/ LIME SLICE ☐

WHAT DO YOU THINK?

. . . .

. . . .

. . . .

. . . .

DRINK THIS AGAIN?   YES ☐   NO ☐   IF DESPERATE ☐

BONUS TRIVIA

IN 1669 THE GERMAN ALCHEMIST HENNIG BRAND, AFTER NOTING
THAT GOLD AND URINE WERE SIMILAR IN COLOR, DEVELOPED
THE BELIEF THAT HE COULD DISTILL THE PRECIOUS METAL FROM
IT. SO HE STARTED COLLECTING URINE, MOSTLY FROM HIS
WIFE AND HER FRIENDS.

AFTER BOILING OVER 1,500 GALLONS OF IT, HE ACTUALLY
DISCOVERED PHOSPHORUS INSTEAD.

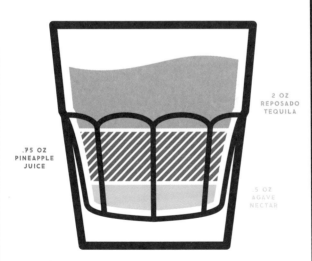

2 OZ
REPOSADO
TEQUILA

.75 OZ
PINEAPPLE
JUICE

.5 OZ
AGAVE
NECTAR

WE'D RECOMMEND A LOWBALL GLASS FOR THIS ONE.

FIRST THINGS FIRST, GO BUY SOME:

▮ HORSERADISH SAUCE

OH. AND YOU'LL ALSO NEED SOME CELERY SALT (AND CELERY)

CHEVY CHASE ORDERS ONE (AND A COUPLE OF STEAK
SANDWICHES) IN THE 1985 MOVIE 'FLETCH.'

INGREDIENTS   INSTRUCTIONS

▮ 2 OZ VODKA   GET SERVING GLASS ☐
▮ 4 DASH WORCESTERSHIRE S.   FILL WITH ICE ☐
▮ .75 OZ LEMON JUICE   ADD FIRST 6 INGREDIENTS ☐
▮ 1 TBSP HORSERADISH S.   TOP W/ TOMATO JUICE ☐
▮ 1 TSP CELERY SALT   STIR TO COMBINE ☐
▮ 4 DASH TABASCO SAUCE   GARNISH W/ CELERY ☐
▮ TOMATO JUICE
▮ CELERY STICK (GARNISH)

WHAT DO YOU THINK?

. . . .

. . . .

DRINK THIS AGAIN?   YES ☐   NO ☐   IF DESPERATE ☐

IT MAKES THE PERFECT AIRLINE COCKTAIL. DUE TO PRESSURE &
ALTITUDE, SWEETS DON'T TASTE AS GOOD. TOMATOES DO.

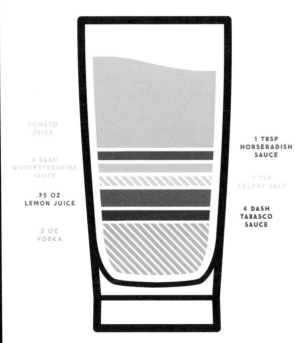

TOMATO
JUICE

4 DASH
WORCESTERSHIRE
SAUCE

.75 OZ
LEMON JUICE

2 OZ
VODKA

1 TBSP
HORSERADISH
SAUCE

1 TSP
CELERY SALT

4 DASH
TABASCO
SAUCE

YOU SHOULD PROBABLY USE A HIGHBALL GLASS.

YOU PRETTY MUCH HAVE EVERYTHING YOU NEED:

■ JUST MAKE SURE YOU HAVE AN EXTRA LEMON

CHECK YOUR BAR FOR ANYTHING YOU'RE GETTING LOW ON. THOUGH

BARRELS ARE DESIGNED TO BE EASILY MOVABLE ON
THEIR SIDES AND TO STAY STATIONARY WHEN UPRIGHT.

INGREDIENTS	INSTRUCTIONS
■ .5 OZ BÉNÉDICTINE	GET MIXING GLASS & ADD ICE ☐
■ 2 OZ RYE WHISKEY	ADD ALL INGREDIENTS ☐
■ 2 DASH ANGOSTURA BITTERS	STIR TO COMBINE ☐
■ .5 OZ AMONTILLADO SHERRY	GET SERVING GLASS ☐
■ LEMON (GARNISH)	FILL WITH ICE ☐
	STRAIN INTO GLASS ☐
	GARNISH W/ LEMON TWIST ☐

WHAT DO YOU THINK?

. . . .

. . . .

. . . .

DRINK THIS AGAIN?   YES ☐   NO ☐   IF DESPERATE ☐

BONUS TRIVIA

THERE'S A SPECIFIC ORDER FOR USING OAK BARRELS. TO BE CLASSIFIED AS BOURBON, IT LEGALLY HAS TO BE AGED IN A NEW OAK BARREL THAT'S BEEN CHARRED. WHISKEY IS AGED IN USED BOURBON BARRELS. SCOTCH IS AGED IN USED WHISKEY BARRELS. RUM IS AGED IN USED SCOTCH BARRELS.

AND TEQUILA IS AGED IN JUST ABOUT ANY OLD BARREL THAT'S LAYING AROUND.

.5 OZ
BÉNÉDICTINE

2 OZ
RYE
WHISKEY

2 DASH
ANGOSTURA
BITTERS

.5 OZ
AMONTILLADO
SHERRY

WE'D RECOMMEND A LOWBALL GLASS FOR THIS ONE.

YOU PRETTY MUCH HAVE EVERYTHING YOU NEED:

JUST MAKE SURE YOU HAVE SOME MINT

AND MAYBE CHECK THE FRESHNESS OF THAT LIME JUICE

A FREE SHOT OF FERNET IS A COMMON 'BARTENDER'S HANDSHAKE' (AKA, A BIT OF BOOZE ON THE HOUSE).

INGREDIENTS

- 2 OZ DARK RUM
- .5 OZ ORGEAT
- .75 OZ LIME JUICE
- .25 OZ FERNET
- MINT SPRIG (GARNISH)

INSTRUCTIONS

- GET SHAKER & FILL W/ ICE ☐
- ADD ALL INGREDIENTS ☐
- SHAKE UNTIL CHILLED ☐
- FILL SERVING GLASS W/ ICE ☐
- STRAIN INTO GLASS ☐
- GARNISH W/ MINT ☐

WHAT DO YOU THINK?

. . . .

. . . .

. . . .

DRINK THIS AGAIN?   YES ☐   NO ☐   IF DESPERATE ☐

BONUS TRIVIA

IN THE 2003 FILM 'PIRATES OF THE CARIBBEAN: THE CURSE OF THE BLACK PEARL,' THERE IS A SMALL SCAB ON THE CHIN OF JACK SPARROW THAT KEEPS GETTING INCREASINGLY LARGER AS THE MOVIE PROGRESSES.

JOHNNY DEPP AND HIS MAKEUP ARTIST DID IT ON PURPOSE AS A PRANK.

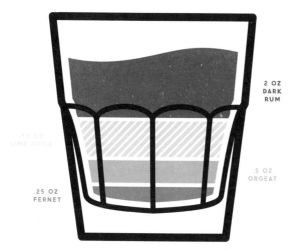

.75 OZ
LIME JUICE

2 OZ
DARK
RUM

.5 OZ
ORGEAT

.25 OZ
FERNET

WE'D RECOMMEND A LOWBALL GLASS FOR THIS ONE.

YOU PRETTY MUCH HAVE EVERYTHING YOU NEED:

SO MAKE A DRINK ALREADY

CHECK YOUR BAR FOR ANYTHING YOU'RE GETTING LOW ON, THOUGH

THE 'STATUE OF JOHN HARVARD' IS ACTUALLY SHERMAN HOAR, A STUDENT MODEL. NO PHOTOS EXIST OF JOHN.

INGREDIENTS	INSTRUCTIONS
1.5 OZ COGNAC	CHILL SERVING GLASS ☐
1 OZ SWEET VERMOUTH	GET MIXING GLASS ☐
3 DASH ANGOSTURA BITTERS	FILL WITH ICE ☐
1 TSP SIMPLE SYRUP	ADD FIRST 4 INGREDIENTS ☐
1 SPLASH CLUB SODA	STIR UNTIL CHILLED ☐
	STRAIN INTO GLASS ☐
	TOP W/ CLUB SODA ☐

WHAT DO YOU THINK?

. . . .

. . . .

. . . .

DRINK THIS AGAIN?   YES ☐   NO ☐   IF DESPERATE ☐

BONUS TRIVIA

HARVARD'S MOTTO IS 'VERITAS' WHICH IS LATIN FOR 'TRUTH.'

1 OZ SWEET VERMOUTH

1 TSP SIMPLE SYRUP

1 SPLASH CLUB SODA

3 DASH ANGOSTURA BITTERS

1.5 OZ COGNAC

GO AHEAD AND GOOGLE WHAT A NICK & NORA GLASS IS.

YOU PRETTY MUCH HAVE EVERYTHING YOU NEED:

JUST MAKE SURE YOU HAVE SOME BRANDIED CHERRIES

MAYBE IT'S TIME TO INVEST IN A NICE BAR CART (YOU DESERVE IT)

CREATED IN 2015 BY TODD SMITH WHILE BARTENDING
AT SAN FRANCISCO'S 'BOURBON & BRANCH.'

INGREDIENTS	INSTRUCTIONS
1 DASH ANGOSTURA BITTERS	GET MIXING GLASS ☐
1 DASH ORANGE BITTERS	FILL WITH ICE ☐
2 OZ RYE WHISKEY	ADD ALL INGREDIENTS ☐
1 OZ CAMPARI	STIR UNTIL CHILLED ☐
BRANDIED CHERRY (GARNISH)	STRAIN INTO GLASS ☐
	GARNISH W/ CHERRY ☐

WHAT DO YOU THINK?

. . . .

. . . .

. . . .

. . . .

DRINK THIS AGAIN? YES ☐ NO ☐ IF DESPERATE ☐

DURING THE 2019 BLACKOUT IN MANHATTAN, NY, A CONCERT
AT CARNEGIE HALL WAS FORCED TO EVACUATE. BUT INSTEAD OF
CANCELING, THE CHOIR PERFORMED ON THE STREET INSTEAD.

2 OZ
RYE
WHISKEY

1 DASH
ORANGE
BITTERS

1 DASH
ANGOSTURA
BITTERS

1 OZ
CAMPARI

USE A COUPE GLASS. TRUST US, IT'S WORTH IT.

YOU PRETTY MUCH HAVE EVERYTHING YOU NEED:

◼ JUST MAKE SURE YOU HAVE AN EXTRA EGG

AND MAYBE CHECK THE FRESHNESS OF THAT LIME JUICE

CREATED BY SIDNEY COX FOR THE 1936 BRITISH EMPIRE
COCKTAIL COMPETITION. IT TOOK FIRST PLACE.

INGREDIENTS

- 1 OZ DRY GIN
- .75 OZ PEACH LIQUEUR
- .75 OZ LEMON JUICE
- 1 EGG WHITE

INSTRUCTIONS

CHILL SERVING GLASS ☐
GET SHAKER & ADD ICE ☐
ADD ALL INGREDIENTS ☐
SHAKE UNTIL CHILLED ☐
STRAIN INTO GLASS ☐

WHAT DO YOU THINK?

. . . .

. . . .

. . . .

. . . .

. . . .

DRINK THIS AGAIN? YES ☐ NO ☐ IF DESPERATE ☐

BONUS TRIVIA

ITS NAME WAS INSPIRED BY KING EDWARD VIII'S 1936 PROPOSAL
TO MARRY WALLIS SIMPSON, THE TWICE-DIVORCED AMERICAN
SOCIALITE. FACED WITH BACKLASH, HE RENOUNCED HIS THRONE
AND MARRIED HIS 'PERFECT LADY' A YEAR LATER.

1 OZ
DRY GIN

.75 OZ
PEACH
LIQUEUR

.75 OZ
LEMON JUICE

1 EGG
WHITE

USE A COUPE GLASS. TRUST US, IT'S WORTH IT.

FIRST THINGS FIRST, GO BUY SOME:

LEMON SODA (SPECIFICALLY, SANPELLEGRINO LIMONATA)

OH, AND YOU'LL ALSO NEED A GRAPEFRUIT

CREATED IN 2013 BY JOHN DERAGON AT 'PLEASE DON'T
TELL' IN THE EAST VILLAGE OF NEW YORK CITY.

INGREDIENTS	INSTRUCTIONS
2 OZ CACHAÇA	GET SHAKER & ADD ICE ☐
.75 OZ LILLET BLANC	ADD FIRST 3 INGREDIENTS ☐
.5 OZ LIME JUICE	SHAKE UNTIL CHILLED ☐
4 OZ LEMON SODA	GET SERVING GLASS ☐
GRAPEFRUIT (GARNISH)	FILL WITH ICE ☐
	STRAIN INTO GLASS ☐
	TOP WITH LEMON SODA ☐
	GARNISH W/ GRAPEFRUIT SLICE ☐

WHAT DO YOU THINK?

. . . .

. . . .

DRINK THIS AGAIN?   YES ☐   NO ☐   IF DESPERATE ☐

BONUS TRIVIA

THE ENTRANCE TO 'PLEASE DON'T TELL' IS HIDDEN IN A PHONE
BOOTH AT 'CRIF DOGS,' A LATE-NIGHT HOT DOG STAND.

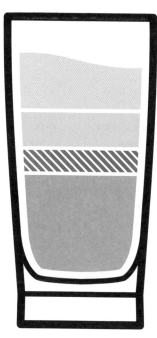

2 OZ
CACHAÇA

.75 OZ
LILLET BLANC

.5 OZ
LIME JUICE

4 OZ
LEMON SODA

YOU SHOULD PROBABLY USE A HIGHBALL GLASS.

YOU PRETTY MUCH HAVE EVERYTHING YOU NEED:

■ JUST MAKE SURE YOU HAVE A LIME OR TWO

AND MAYBE CHECK THE FRESHNESS OF THAT LIME JUICE

THE NATIONAL SIESTA CHAMPIONSHIP, A NAPPING COMPETITION, IS HELD IN MADRID EVERY YEAR.

INGREDIENTS

- 2 OZ BLANCO TEQUILA
- .5 OZ LIME JUICE
- .5 OZ GRAPEFRUIT JUICE
- .5 OZ SIMPLE SYRUP
- .5 OZ CAMPARI
- LIME (GARNISH)

INSTRUCTIONS

- GET SHAKER & ADD ICE ☐
- ADD ALL INGREDIENTS ☐
- SHAKE UNTIL CHILLED ☐
- STRAIN INTO GLASS ☐
- GARNISH W/ LIME SLICE ☐

WHAT DO YOU THINK?

. . . .

. . . .

. . . .

DRINK THIS AGAIN?   YES ☐   NO ☐   IF DESPERATE ☐

MAKE A SIESTA

2 OZ
BLANCO
TEQUILA

.5 OZ
LIME JUICE

.5 OZ
GRAPEFRUIT
JUICE

.5 OZ
CAMPARI

.5 OZ
SIMPLE
SYRUP

THIS ONE LOOKS GREAT IN A MARTINI GLASS.

YOU PRETTY MUCH HAVE EVERYTHING YOU NEED:

■ JUST PICK UP SOME CARAWAY SEEDS

■ AND MAYBE CHECK THE FRESHNESS OF THOSE JUICES

> ZEPHYRUS, THE GOD OF THE WEST WIND, EVENTUALLY
> EVOLVED INTO ZEPHYR, A WORD FOR A SOFT BREEZE.

INGREDIENTS	INSTRUCTIONS
■ .75 OZ ABSINTHE	GET SERVING GLASS ☐
■ .5 OZ ORGEAT	FILL WITH ICE ☐
■ .5 OZ VODKA	ADD ALL INGREDIENTS ☐
■ .5 OZ GRAPEFRUIT JUICE	STIR TO COMBINE ☐
■ .25 OZ LEMON JUICE	GARNISH W/ SEEDS ☐
■ 3 DASH PEYCHAUD'S BITTERS	
■ CARAWAY SEEDS (GARNISH)	

WHAT DO YOU THINK?

. . . .

. . . .

. . . .

. . . .

DRINK THIS AGAIN?   YES ☐   NO ☐   IF DESPERATE ☐

BONUS TRIVIA

THE LONGEST MAJOR LEAGUE BASEBALL GAME IN HISTORY WAS PLAYED ON MAY 8TH (AND 9TH) OF 1984, AT COMINSKY PARK IN CHICAGO. AFTER 25 INNINGS OF PLAY, TAKING 8 HOURS AND 6 MINUTES TO COMPLETE, THE WHITE SOX DEFEATED THE MILWAUKEE BREWERS, 7 TO 6.

BUT HONESTLY, IT KIND OF SOUNDS LIKE EVERYBODY LOST.

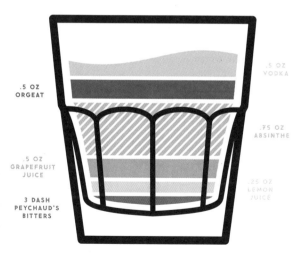

.5 OZ ORGEAT

.5 OZ VODKA

.75 OZ ABSINTHE

.5 OZ GRAPEFRUIT JUICE

.25 OZ LEMON JUICE

3 DASH PEYCHAUD'S BITTERS

WE'D RECOMMEND A LOWBALL GLASS FOR THIS ONE.

FIRST THINGS FIRST, GO BUY SOME:

COLD BREW COFFEE (YOU CAN BUY IT, OR MAKE IT)

OH, AND YOU'LL ALSO NEED A LEMON

COLD BREW IS MADE BY STEEPING COFFEE BEANS IN
COLD WATER FOR 12 HOURS TO EXTRACT THE FLAVOR.*

INGREDIENTS	INSTRUCTIONS
1.5 OZ ELDERFLOWER LIQUEUR	GET SERVING GLASS ☐
2 OZ COLD BREW COFFEE	FILL WITH ICE ☐
.75 OZ FERNET	ADD FIRST 3 INGREDIENTS ☐
4 OZ TONIC WATER	STIR UNTIL CHILLED ☐
LEMON (GARNISH)	TOP W/ TONIC WATER ☐
	GARNISH W/ LEMON TWIST ☐

WHAT DO YOU THINK?

. . . .

. . . .

. . . .

*WHEREAS ICED COFFEE IS JUST BREWED COFFEE POURED OVER ICE.

DRINK THIS AGAIN?   YES ☐   NO ☐   IF DESPERATE ☐

BONUS TRIVIA

CREATED BY THE 2015 AMERICAN BARTENDER OF THE YEAR, IVY MIX. SHE ALSO POPULARIZED MEZCAL IN THE U.S., NO BIG DEAL.

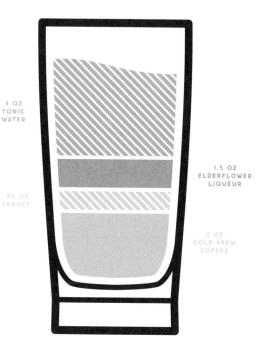

4 OZ
TONIC
WATER

1.5 OZ
ELDERFLOWER
LIQUEUR

.75 OZ
FERNET

2 OZ
COLD BREW
COFFEE

YOU SHOULD PROBABLY USE A HIGHBALL GLASS.

YOU PRETTY MUCH HAVE EVERYTHING YOU NEED:

JUST MAKE SURE YOU HAVE SOME BRANDIED CHERRIES

AND MAYBE CHECK THE FRESHNESS OF THAT VERMOUTH

CREATED IN 1894 AT NYC'S WALDORF-ASTORIA HOTEL.
IT'S GONE; THE EMPIRE STATE BUILDING IS THERE NOW.

INGREDIENTS

- 2 OZ SCOTCH
- .75 OZ SWEET VERMOUTH
- 3 DASH ANGOSTURA BITTERS
- BRANDIED CHERRY (GARNISH)

INSTRUCTIONS

- CHILL SERVING GLASS ☐
- GET MIXING GLASS ☐
- FILL WITH ICE ☐
- ADD ALL INGREDIENTS ☐
- STIR UNTIL CHILLED ☐
- STRAIN INTO GLASS ☐
- GARNISH W/ CHERRY ☐

WHAT DO YOU THINK?

. . . .

. . . .

. . . .

DRINK THIS AGAIN?   YES ☐   NO ☐   IF DESPERATE ☐

BONUS TRIVIA

IT'S NOT NAMED AFTER ROB ROY MACGREGOR, THE SCOTTISH FOLK HERO. IT'S NAMED AFTER THE PLAY THAT'S NAMED AFTER HIM.

3 DASH
ANGOSTURA
BITTERS

.75 OZ
SWEET
VERMOUTH

2 OZ
SCOTCH

YOU COULD ALSO USE A COUPE. IT'S YOUR CALL.

YOU PRETTY MUCH HAVE EVERYTHING YOU NEED:

☐ JUST MAKE SURE YOU HAVE AN EXTRA ORANGE

CHECK YOUR BAR FOR ANYTHING YOU'RE GETTING LOW ON, THOUGH

THIS DRINK PREDATES THE FORD MOTOR COMPANY
BY 8 YEARS (AND GERALD FORD BY 18).

INGREDIENTS

INSTRUCTIONS

1 OZ DRY GIN — CHILL SERVING GLASS ☐

1 OZ DRY VERMOUTH — GET MIXING GLASS ☐

.25 OZ BÉNÉDICTINE — FILL WITH ICE ☐

3 DASH ORANGE BITTERS — ADD ALL INGREDIENTS ☐

ORANGE (GARNISH) — STIR UNTIL CHILLED ☐

STRAIN INTO GLASS ☐

GARNISH W/ ORANGE TWIST ☐

WHAT DO YOU THINK?

. . . .

. . . .

DRINK THIS AGAIN?   YES ☐   NO ☐   IF DESPERATE ☐

HENRY FORD, AN OUTSPOKEN PROHIBITIONIST, ONCE DECLARED
THAT 'NOBODY CAN DRINK ALCOHOL & SMOKE WITHOUT INJURING
THEIR BRAINS.' WELL THIS ONE'S FOR YOU, HENRY.

1 OZ
DRY GIN

3 DASH
ORANGE
BITTERS

.25 OZ
BÉNÉDICTINE

1 OZ DRY
VERMOUTH

USE A COUPE GLASS. TRUST US, IT'S WORTH IT.

YOU PRETTY MUCH HAVE EVERYTHING YOU NEED:

■ JUST MAKE SURE YOU HAVE AN ORANGE

OH, AND YOU'LL ALSO NEED A BRANDIED CHERRY

FIRST MADE BY DONN BEACH, THE 'FOUNDING FATHER'
OF THE TIKI FAD OF THE 1940s AND 50s.

INGREDIENTS

■ 1 OZ WHITE RUM
■ 1 OZ DARK RUM
■ 1 OZ HONEY SYRUP
■ .75 OZ GRAPEFRUIT JUICE
■ .75 OZ CLUB SODA
■ BRANDIED CHERRY (GARNISH)
■ ORANGE (GARNISH)

INSTRUCTIONS

GET SHAKER ☐
FILL WITH ICE ☐
ADD FIRST 4 INGREDIENTS ☐
SHAKE UNTIL CHILLED ☐
GET SERVING GLASS ☐
FILL WITH ICE ☐
STRAIN INTO GLASS ☐
GARNISH W/ ORANGE SLICE ☐
ADD BRANDIED CHERRY ☐

WHAT DO YOU THINK?

. . . .

DRINK THIS AGAIN?   YES ☐   NO ☐   IF DESPERATE ☐

BONUS TRIVIA

REPORTEDLY, PHIL SPECTOR DRANK AT LEAST 2 NAVY GROGS
AT TRADER VIC'S BEVERLY HILTON RESTAURANT, WITHOUT
HAVING ANY FOOD, THE NIGHT HE LATER (ALLEGEDLY)
KILLED ACTRESS LANA CLARKSON IN 2003.

BE SAFE, MAYBE EAT A FEW TACOS OR SOMETHING.

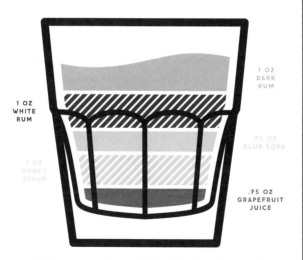

1 OZ
DARK
RUM

1 OZ
WHITE
RUM

.75 OZ
CLUB SODA

1 OZ
HONEY
SYRUP

.75 OZ
GRAPEFRUIT
JUICE

WE'D RECOMMEND A LOWBALL GLASS FOR THIS ONE.

FIRST THINGS FIRST, GO BUY SOME:

PISCO (IT'S $\overline{\text{PEE}}$-SKOW. YEAH, WE KNOW. GROW UP.)

OH, AND MAKE SURE YOU HAVE FRESH GINGER BEER (AND A LIME)

CHILCANO IS ALSO THE NAME OF A POPULAR PERUVIAN FISH HEAD SOUP, APTLY KNOWN AS A HANGOVER CURE.

INGREDIENTS

2 OZ PISCO
.25 OZ LIME JUICE
4 OZ GINGER BEER
LIME (GARNISH)

INSTRUCTIONS

GET SERVING GLASS ☐
FILL WITH ICE ☐
ADD ALL INGREDIENTS ☐
STIR UNTIL CHILLED ☐
GARNISH W/ LIME TWIST ☐

WHAT DO YOU THINK?

. . . .

. . . .

. . . .

. . . .

DRINK THIS AGAIN?   YES ☐   NO ☐   IF DESPERATE ☐

BONUS TRIVIA

WHILE WE'RE REFERRING TO PERUVIAN PISCO, A DIFFERENT SPIRIT (ALSO CALLED PISCO) IS MADE IN CHILE. THEY FIGHT. A LOT.

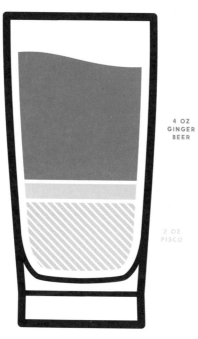

4 OZ
GINGER
BEER

.25 OZ
LIME JUICE

2 OZ
PISCO

YOU SHOULD PROBABLY USE A HIGHBALL GLASS.

YOU PRETTY MUCH HAVE EVERYTHING YOU NEED:

▮ JUST MAKE SURE YOU HAVE A LIME

▬ AND MAYBE CHECK THE FRESHNESS OF THAT GINGER BEER

THE FIRST KNOWN APPEARANCE OF THIS COCKTAIL WAS
IN 'TRADER VIC'S BOOK OF FOOD AND DRINK' IN 1946.

INGREDIENTS

- 1.5 OZ REPOSADO TEQUILA
- .5 OZ CRÈME DE CASSIS
- .5 OZ LIME JUICE
- 3 OZ GINGER BEER
- LIME (GARNISH)

INSTRUCTIONS

- GET SHAKER ☐
- FILL WITH ICE ☐
- ADD FIRST 3 INGREDIENTS ☐
- SHAKE UNTIL CHILLED ☐
- STRAIN INTO SERVING GLASS ☐
- GARNISH W/ LIME WEDGE ☐

WHAT DO YOU THINK?

. . . .

. . . .

. . . .

DRINK THIS AGAIN?   YES ☐   NO ☐   IF DESPERATE ☐

BONUS TRIVIA

YOU CAN SEE MORE OF THE EARTH'S SURFACE FROM THE PEAK OF
MOUNT DIABLO (IN CA) THAN AT ANY OTHER SPOT IN THE U.S.

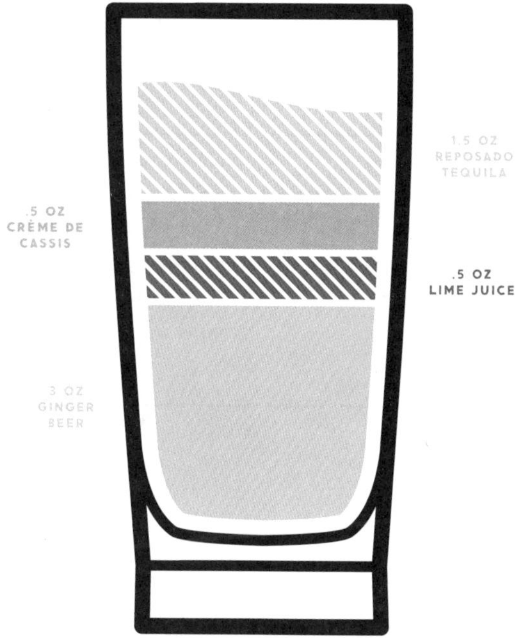

1.5 OZ
REPOSADO
TEQUILA

.5 OZ
CRÈME DE
CASSIS

.5 OZ
LIME JUICE

3 OZ
GINGER
BEER

THIS ONE LOOKS GREAT IN A HIGHBALL GLASS.

YOU PRETTY MUCH HAVE EVERYTHING YOU NEED:

■ JUST MAKE SURE YOU HAVE AN EXTRA LEMON

AND MAYBE CHECK THE FRESHNESS OF THAT LEMON JUICE

ITS NAME IS A REFERENCE TO THE 2007 M.I.A. SONG
'PAPER PLANES,' A FAVORITE OF THE CREATORS.

INGREDIENTS

- .75 OZ BOURBON
- .75 OZ ANISETTE LIQUEUR
- .75 OZ CAMPARI
- .75 OZ LEMON JUICE
- LEMON (GARNISH)

INSTRUCTIONS

- CHILL SERVING GLASS ☐
- GET SHAKER & ADD ICE ☐
- ADD ALL INGREDIENTS ☐
- SHAKE UNTIL CHILLED ☐
- STRAIN INTO GLASS ☐
- GARNISH W/ LEMON TWIST ☐

WHAT DO YOU THINK?

. . . .

. . . .

. . . .

DRINK THIS AGAIN?   YES ☐   NO ☐   IF DESPERATE ☐

BONUS TRIVIA

ON FEBRUARY 26TH, 2012, JOE AYOOB AND JOHN COLLINS SET THE CURRENT WORLD RECORD FOR THE LONGEST THROW OF A PAPER AIRPLANE — 226 FEET, 10 INCHES.

.75 OZ CAMPARI

.75 OZ BOURBON

.75 OZ LEMON JUICE

.75 OZ ANISETTE LIQUEUR

USE A COUPE GLASS. TRUST US, IT'S WORTH IT.

FIRST THINGS FIRST, GO BUY SOME:

☐ CITRUS VODKA

OH, AND YOU'LL ALSO NEED TO HAVE SOME SUGAR

THE STOCKHOLM SUBWAY IS KNOWN AS THE WORLD'S LONGEST ART GALLERY. NYC'S? THE LONGEST BATHROOM.

INGREDIENTS	INSTRUCTIONS
.75 OZ CITRUS VODKA	GET SERVING GLASS ☐
.75 OZ SIMPLE SYRUP	RIM W/ LEMON JUICE ☐
.75 OZ LEMON JUICE	DIP IN SUGAR ☐
3 OZ CHAMPAGNE	GET SHAKER & ADD ICE ☐
SUGAR (RIM OF GLASS)	ADD FIRST 3 INGREDIENTS ☐
	SHAKE UNTIL CHILLED ☐
	STRAIN INTO GLASS ☐
	TOP WITH CHAMPAGNE ☐

WHAT DO YOU THINK?

. . . .

. . . .

DRINK THIS AGAIN?   YES ☐   NO ☐   IF DESPERATE ☐

BONUS TRIVIA

STOCKHOLM SYNDROME IS NAMED AFTER A 1973 ROBBERY IN
WHICH THE HOSTAGES LATER DEFENDED THEIR CAPTORS.

.75 OZ
SIMPLE SYRUP

.75 OZ
CITRUS VODKA

.75 OZ
LEMON JUICE

3 OZ
CHAMPAGNE

THIS ONE DEFINITELY CALLS FOR A MARTINI GLASS.

YOU PRETTY MUCH HAVE EVERYTHING YOU NEED:

■ PEDRO XIMÉNEZ SHERRY (ALSO KNOWN AS PX SHERRY)

OH, AND YOU'LL ALSO NEED A LEMON

THE CHEMICAL SYMBOL FOR GOLD IS AU, FROM THE
LATIN WORD 'AURUM' MEANING 'SHINING DAWN.'

INGREDIENTS	INSTRUCTIONS
■ 2 OZ BOURBON	GET MIXING GLASS & ADD ICE ☐
■ .75 OZ CAMPARI	ADD ALL INGREDIENTS ☐
■ .5 OZ PEDRO XIMÉNEZ SHERRY	STIR UNTIL CHILLED ☐
■ LEMON (GARNISH)	STRAIN INTO GLASS ☐
	GARNISH W/ LEMON TWIST ☐

WHAT DO YOU THINK?

. . . .

. . . .

. . . .

. . . .

DRINK THIS AGAIN?   YES ☐   NO ☐   IF DESPERATE ☐

BONUS TRIVIA

SAMUEL CLEMENS (AKA MARK TWAIN) ONLY GOT INTO WRITING
BECAUSE HE FAILED TO MAKE A LIVING AS A PROSPECTOR.

2 OZ
BOURBON

.75 OZ
CAMPARI

.5 OZ
PEDRO
XIMÉNEZ
SHERRY

USE A COUPE GLASS. TRUST US, IT'S WORTH IT.

FIRST THINGS FIRST, GO BUY SOME:

STOUT BEER (PICK YOUR FAVORITE)

OH, AND YOU'LL ALSO NEED SOME CREAM (AND CINNAMON)

IN 1759, ARTHUR GUINNESS SIGNED A 9,000-YEAR LEASE
FOR HIS BREWERY. IT STILL COSTS THEM £45 A MONTH.

INGREDIENTS

- 2 OZ COLD BREW COFFEE
- 2 OZ STOUT BEER
- 1.5 OZ IRISH WHISKEY
- .75 OZ SIMPLE SYRUP
- .5 OZ CREAM
- CINNAMON (GARNISH)

INSTRUCTIONS

- GET SERVING GLASS ☐
- FILL WITH ICE ☐
- ADD FIRST 4 INGREDIENTS ☐
- STIR TO COMBINE ☐
- GENTLY POUR IN CREAM ☐
- GARNISH W/ CINNAMON ☐

WHAT DO YOU THINK?

. . . .

. . . .

. . . .

DRINK THIS AGAIN?   YES ☐   NO ☐   IF DESPERATE ☐

BONUS TRIVIA

DUBLIN'S OLDEST KNOWN PUB IS 'THE BRAZEN HEAD.' ORIGINALLY
A COACH HOUSE, IT WAS TURNED INTO A PUBLIC HOUSE IN 1198.

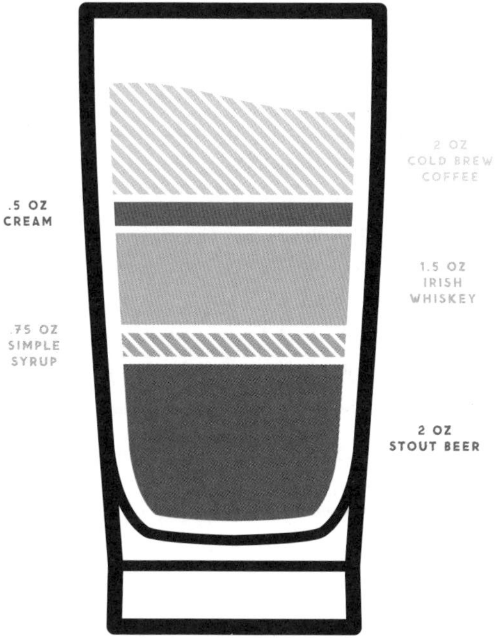

2 OZ
COLD BREW
COFFEE

.5 OZ
CREAM

1.5 OZ
IRISH
WHISKEY

.75 OZ
SIMPLE
SYRUP

2 OZ
STOUT BEER

THIS ONE LOOKS GREAT IN A HIGHBALL GLASS.

FIRST THINGS FIRST, GO BUY SOME:

COCONUT RUM

AND MAYBE CHECK THE FRESHNESS OF THOSE JUICES

SPOILER ALERT: THAT'S NOT COURAGE THAT YOU'RE
FEELING. IT'S JUST YOUR LIVER CRYING FOR HELP.

INGREDIENTS   **INSTRUCTIONS**

1.5 OZ TENNESSEE WHISKEY   GET SHAKER ☐
1.5 OZ AMARETTO   FILL WITH ICE ☐
1.5 OZ COCONUT RUM   ADD FIRST 4 INGREDIENTS ☐
1.5 OZ CURAÇAO   SHAKE TO COMBINE ☐
2 OZ ORANGE JUICE   ADD ALL JUICES ☐
2 OZ CRANBERRY JUICE   SHAKE UNTIL CHILLED ☐
2 OZ PINEAPPLE JUICE   GET SERVING GLASS ☐
                                        FILL WITH ICE ☐
                                     STRAIN INTO GLASS ☐

WHAT DO YOU THINK?

. . . .

DRINK THIS AGAIN?   YES ☐   NO ☐   IF DESPERATE ☐

BONUS TRIVIA

THE WORD COURAGE ORIGINATES FROM THE OLD FRENCH
'CORAGE,' MEANING 'HEART AND SPIRIT.'

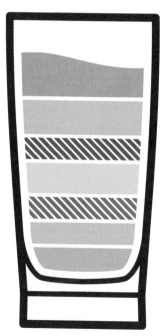

2 OZ
PINEAPPLE
JUICE

2 OZ
CRANBERRY
JUICE

1.5 OZ
CURAÇAO

2 OZ
ORANGE
JUICE

1.5 OZ
TENNESSEE
WHISKEY

1.5 OZ
AMARETTO

1.5 OZ
COCONUT
RUM

YOU SHOULD PROBABLY USE A HIGHBALL GLASS.

YOU PRETTY MUCH HAVE EVERYTHING YOU NEED:

JUST MAKE SURE YOUR GRAPEFRUIT JUICE IS STILL GOOD

OH, AND YOU'LL ALSO NEED A GRAPEFRUIT

THE GRAPEFRUIT RECEIVED ITS NAME FROM THE WAY
THAT THE FRUIT GROWS IN BUNCHES LIKE GRAPES DO.

INGREDIENTS

INSTRUCTIONS

2 OZ REPOSADO TEQUILA

1 OZ ANISETTE LIQUEUR

2 OZ GRAPEFRUIT JUICE

GRAPEFRUIT (GARNISH)

GET SHAKER & ADD ICE ☐

ADD ALL INGREDIENTS ☐

SHAKE UNTIL CHILLED ☐

GET SERVING GLASS ☐

FILL WITH ICE ☐

STRAIN INTO GLASS ☐

GARNISH W/ GRAPEFRUIT TWIST ☐

WHAT DO YOU THINK?

. . . .

. . . .

. . . .

. . . .

DRINK THIS AGAIN?   YES ☐   NO ☐   IF DESPERATE ☐

BONUS TRIVIA

THIS COCKTAIL WAS CREATED IN 2008 BY AISHA SHARPE AND WILLY SHINE AT 'CONTEMPORARY COCKTAILS' IN NEW YORK CITY.

THE NAME OF THE DRINK, WHILE BEING A REFERENCE TO THE MANHATTAN AREA CODE, ALSO HAPPENS TO BE THE RATIOS USED IN THE RECIPE.

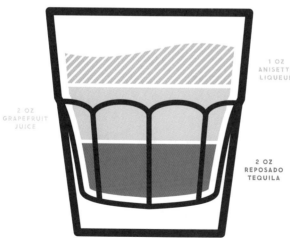

1 OZ
ANISETTE
LIQUEUR

2 OZ
GRAPEFRUIT
JUICE

2 OZ
REPOSADO
TEQUILA

WE'D RECOMMEND A LOWBALL GLASS FOR THIS ONE.

YOU PRETTY MUCH HAVE EVERYTHING YOU NEED:

◼ YOU'RE WELCOME

WE ACCEPT 'DONATIONS' AT BRASSMONKEYGOODS.COM

ORIGINALLY CREATED IN 1861 TO MOURN THE DEATH OF
QUEEN VICTORIA'S HUSBAND — PRINCE ALBERT.

INGREDIENTS

◼ 4 OZ CHAMPAGNE
◼ 2 OZ STOUT BEER

INSTRUCTIONS

GET SERVING GLASS ☐
ADD CHAMPAGNE ☐
FLOAT* STOUT ON TOP ☐
DO NOT STIR ☐

WHAT DO YOU THINK?

. . . .

. . . .

. . . .

. . . .

. . . .

*IF YOU'VE FORGOTTEN HOW, CHECK OUT DRINK 52.

DRINK THIS AGAIN?   YES ☐   NO ☐   IF DESPERATE ☐

MAKE A BLACK VELVET

4 OZ
CHAMPAGNE

2 OZ
STOUT BEER

FINALLY, A USE FOR THOSE CHAMPAGNE FLUTES.

YOU PRETTY MUCH HAVE EVERYTHING YOU NEED:

JUST MAKE SURE YOUR ORANGE JUICE IS STILL FRESH

CHECK YOUR BAR FOR ANYTHING YOU'RE GETTING LOW ON, THOUGH

THE LAYERS OF THIS DRINK LOOK LIKE A SUNSET, BUT
THE AMARETTO IS WHAT MAKES IT SO 'ITALIAN.'

INGREDIENTS

- 2 OZ AMARETTO
- 3 OZ ORANGE JUICE
- 3 OZ CLUB SODA
- 1 DASH GRENADINE

INSTRUCTIONS

- GET SERVING GLASS ☐
- FILL WITH ICE ☐
- POUR IN AMARETTO ☐
- FLOAT* ORANGE JUICE ☐
- FLOAT* CLUB SODA ON TOP ☐
- ADD DASH OF GRENADINE ☐
- DO NOT STIR ☐

WHAT DO YOU THINK?

. . . .

. . . .

*YOU JUST DID THIS. BUT IF YOU FORGOT HOW—CHECK OUT DRINK 52.

DRINK THIS AGAIN?   YES ☐   NO ☐   IF DESPERATE ☐

MAKE AN ITALIAN SUNSET

THERE'S A DRINKING FOUNTAIN IN CENTRAL ITALY THAT DISPENSES RED WINE 24 HOURS A DAY, AND IT'S FREE TO EVERYONE.

3 OZ
CLUB SODA

3 OZ
ORANGE
JUICE

1 DASH
GRENADINE

2 OZ
AMARETTO

YOU SHOULD PROBABLY USE A HIGHBALL GLASS.

YOU PRETTY MUCH HAVE EVERYTHING YOU NEED:

JUST MAKE SURE YOU HAVE AN EXTRA EGG

CHECK YOUR BAR FOR ANYTHING YOU'RE GETTING LOW ON, THOUGH

FIRST CREATED IN 1916 BY VICTOR MORRIS, AN AMERICAN WHO HAD MOVED TO PERU FOR THE MINING TRADE.

INGREDIENTS	INSTRUCTIONS
3 OZ PISCO	GET SHAKER ☐
1 OZ LIME JUICE	ADD FIRST 4 INGREDIENTS ☐
.75 OZ SIMPLE SYRUP	DRY SHAKE UNTIL FOAMY ☐
1 EGG WHITE	FILL WITH ICE ☐
4 DASH ANGOSTURA BITTERS	SHAKE AGAIN ☐
	GET SERVING GLASS ☐
	FILL WITH ICE ☐
	STRAIN INTO GLASS ☐
	ADD ANGOSTURA BITTERS ☐

WHAT DO YOU THINK?

. . . .

DRINK THIS AGAIN?   YES ☐   NO ☐   IF DESPERATE ☐

BONUS TRIVIA

IN 2003, THE PERUVIAN GOVERNMENT ESTABLISHED AN OFFICIAL 'NATIONAL PISCO SOUR DAY,' TO BE CELEBRATED ANNUALLY ON THE FIRST IN FEBRUARY.

TO CLOSE OUT THE DAY, PERUVIANS ARE ENCOURAGED TO FINISH A PISCO SOUR BEFORE THE END OF THEIR NATIONAL ANTHEM (AROUND 2 MINUTES AND 30 SECONDS).

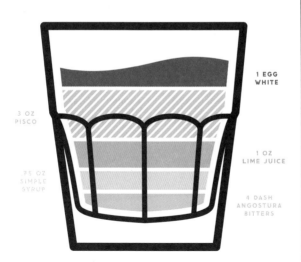

1 EGG WHITE

3 OZ PISCO

1 OZ LIME JUICE

.75 OZ SIMPLE SYRUP

4 DASH ANGOSTURA BITTERS

WE'D RECOMMEND A LOWBALL GLASS FOR THIS ONE.

FIRST THINGS FIRST, GO BUY SOME:

▨ ALLSPICE DRAM

OH, AND MAKE SURE YOU HAVE AN EXTRA ORANGE

LAWN DARTS WERE OFFICIALLY BANNED IN THE U.S.
IN 1988, AFTER SENDING THOUSANDS TO THE ER.

INGREDIENTS

▨ 1 DASH ORANGE BITTERS
▨ 1 DASH ALLSPICE DRAM
▨ 2 OZ BOURBON
▨ .5 OZ ORGEAT
▨ .5 OZ LEMON JUICE
▨ .25 OZ SIMPLE SYRUP
▨ .25 OZ FERNET
▨ ORANGE (GARNISH)

INSTRUCTIONS

GET SHAKER ☐
ADD ALL INGREDIENTS ☐
DRY SHAKE FOR 1 MINUTE ☐
ADD ICE & SHAKE AGAIN ☐
STRAIN INTO GLASS ☐
GARNISH W/ ORANGE SLICE ☐

WHAT DO YOU THINK?

. . . .

. . . .

DRINK THIS AGAIN?   YES ☐   NO ☐   IF DESPERATE ☐

BONUS TRIVIA

THE POISON DART FROG WAS GIVEN ITS NAME BY THE NATIVE AMERICANS. THEY USED ITS TOXIN TO POISON THEIR BLOW DARTS FOR HUNTING.

2 OZ BOURBON

.5 OZ ORGEAT

.25 OZ FERNET

1 DASH ALLSPICE DRAM

.5 OZ LEMON JUICE

.25 OZ SIMPLE SYRUP

1 DASH ORANGE BITTERS

USE A COUPE GLASS. TRUST US, IT'S WORTH IT.

YOU PRETTY MUCH HAVE EVERYTHING YOU NEED:

■ SO MAKE A DRINK ALREADY

CHECK YOUR BAR FOR ANYTHING YOU'RE GETTING LOW ON, THOUGH

THIS DRINK, NAMED AFTER THE 1971 GENE HACKMAN
FILM, FIRST APPEARED IN THE EARLY 1970s.

INGREDIENTS	INSTRUCTIONS
■ 2 OZ COGNAC	GET SERVING GLASS & ADD ICE ☐
■ 2 OZ AMARETTO	ADD ALL INGREDIENTS ☐
	STIR TO COMBINE ☐

WHAT DO YOU THINK?

. . . .

. . . .

. . . .

. . . .

. . . .

DRINK THIS AGAIN? YES ☐ NO ☐ IF DESPERATE ☐

BONUS TRIVIA

THE FILM 'THE FRENCH CONNECTION' IS BASED ON AN ACTUAL 1961 DRUG BUST MADE BY TWO NEW YORK COPS, EDDIE EGAN & SONNY GROSSO. THE ARREST NETTED 112 POUNDS OF HEROIN WITH A STREET VALUE (AT THE TIME) OF OVER $32 MILLION.

SPOILER ALERT: THE REAL CASE WAS NOWHERE NEAR AS VIOLENT AS THE FILM. EGAN SAYS THAT HE ONLY FIRED HIS GUN 3 TIMES...IN HIS CAREER.

2 OZ
COGNAC

2 OZ
AMARETTO

WE'D RECOMMEND A LOWBALL GLASS FOR THIS ONE.

YOU PRETTY MUCH HAVE EVERYTHING YOU NEED:

JUST MAKE SURE YOUR LEMON JUICE IS FRESH

OH, AND YOU'LL ALSO NEED AN ACTUAL LEMON

NAMED AFTER THE MOST VISITED STREET IN PARIS
(OVER 300,000 PEOPLE WALK DOWN IT EVERY DAY).

INGREDIENTS

- 1.25 OZ BRANDY
- 1 DASH ANGOSTURA BITTERS
- .5 OZ GREEN CHARTREUSE
- .5 OZ SIMPLE SYRUP
- .5 OZ LEMON JUICE
- LEMON (GARNISH)

INSTRUCTIONS

- GET SHAKER & ADD ICE ☐
- ADD ALL INGREDIENTS ☐
- SHAKE UNTIL CHILLED ☐
- STRAIN INTO GLASS ☐
- GARNISH W/ LEMON TWIST ☐

WHAT DO YOU THINK?

. . . .

. . . .

. . . .

. . . .

DRINK THIS AGAIN?   YES ☐   NO ☐   IF DESPERATE ☐

BONUS TRIVIA

'CHAMPS-ÉLYSÉES' MEANS 'ELYSIAN FIELDS.' ACCORDING TO GREEK MYTHOLOGY, THE ELYSIAN FIELDS ARE A RESTING PLACE, A PARADISE AFTER DEATH FOR HEROES THAT HAVE PASSED ON.

1.25 OZ
BRANDY

.5 OZ
SIMPLE
SYRUP

.5 OZ
LEMON
JUICE

1 DASH
ANGOSTURA
BITTERS

.5 OZ
GREEN
CHARTREUSE

USE A COUPE GLASS. TRUST US, IT'S WORTH IT.

YOU PRETTY MUCH HAVE EVERYTHING YOU NEED:

JUST MAKE SURE YOU HAVE SOME MINT

AND MAYBE CHECK THE FRESHNESS OF THAT LIME JUICE

IN 2012, THE ADULT LITERACY RATE (AKA PEOPLE OVER THE AGE OF 14) IN CUBA WAS 99.8 PERCENT.

INGREDIENTS	INSTRUCTIONS
5 MINT LEAVES	GET SHAKER ☐
1 OZ SIMPLE SYRUP	ADD FIRST 2 INGREDIENTS ☐
.75 OZ LIME JUICE	MUDDLE TO MIX ☐
2 DASH ANGOSTURA BITTERS	FILL WITH ICE ☐
1.5 OZ DARK RUM	ADD OTHER INGREDIENTS ☐
2 OZ PROSECCO	SHAKE UNTIL CHILLED ☐
MINT SPRIG (GARNISH)	STRAIN INTO GLASS ☐
	GARNISH W/ MINT SPRIG ☐

WHAT DO YOU THINK?

. . . .

. . . .

DRINK THIS AGAIN?   YES ☐   NO ☐   IF DESPERATE ☐

BONUS TRIVIA

THE CUBAN SANDWICH ACTUALLY ORIGINATED IN THE YBOR CITY
AREA OF TAMPA, FL, IN THE LATE 1800s. WHILE NAMED AFTER THE
CUBAN IMMIGRANTS THAT SETTLED THERE, THE INGREDIENTS ARE
A NOD TO THE ITALIANS & GERMANS IN THE NEIGHBORHOOD.

.75 OZ
LIME
JUICE

1.5 OZ
DARK
RUM

2 OZ
PROSECCO

2 DASH
ANGOSTURA
BITTERS

1 OZ
SIMPLE SYRUP

THIS ONE LOOKS GREAT IN A COUPE GLASS.

YOU PRETTY MUCH HAVE EVERYTHING YOU NEED:

JUST MAKE SURE YOU HAVE A LEMON

AND MAYBE CHECK THE FRESHNESS OF THAT GINGER BEER

THE STATE OF RHODE ISLAND IS ONLY 37 MILES WIDE
(AND A WHOPPING 48 MILES TALL).

INGREDIENTS	INSTRUCTIONS
1.5 OZ RASPBERRY LIQUEUR	GET SHAKER ☐
2 OZ BLANCO TEQUILA	FILL WITH ICE ☐
.75 OZ LEMON JUICE	ADD FIRST 5 INGREDIENTS ☐
.5 OZ AGAVE NECTAR	SHAKE UNTIL CHILLED ☐
1 DASH ORANGE BITTERS	FILL GLASS W/ ICE ☐
1 SPLASH GINGER BEER	STRAIN INTO GLASS ☐
LEMON (GARNISH)	TOP WITH GINGER BEER ☐
	GARNISH W/ LEMON TWIST ☐

WHAT DO YOU THINK?

. . . .

. . . .

DRINK THIS AGAIN?   YES ☐   NO ☐   IF DESPERATE ☐

MAKE A RHODE ISLAND RED

THIS DRINK IS NAMED AFTER THE STATE BIRD OF RHODE ISLAND,
A BREED OF CHICKEN THAT ISN'T EVEN NATIVE TO THE U.S.

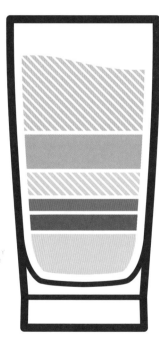

2 OZ
BLANCO
TEQUILA

.75 OZ
LEMON
JUICE

5 OZ
AGAVE
NECTAR

1 DASH
ORANGE
BITTERS

1 SPLASH
GINGER
BEER

1.5 OZ
RASPBERRY
LIQUEUR

YOU SHOULD PROBABLY USE A HIGHBALL GLASS.

MAKE A DRUNKEN DRAWING

PROMPT:

YOUR LIFE BEFORE OWNING THIS BOOK.

MAKE A DRUNKEN DRAWING

PROMPT:

YOUR LIFE AFTER COMPLETING IT.

TABLE OF COCKTAILS

TABLE OF COCKTAILS

TABLE OF COCKTAILS

TABLE OF COCKTAILS

TABLE OF COCKTAILS